Psychological Testing and Assessment

SIXTH EDITION

Psychological Testing and Assessment

LEWIS R. AIKEN
Pepperdine University

ALLYN AND BACON, INC.
Boston London Sydney Toronto

A Division of Simon & Schuster
7 Wells Avenue, Newton, Massachusetts 02159

The first edition was published under the title, *Psychological and Educational Testing,* Copyright © 1971 by Allyn and Bacon, Inc.

Library of Congress Cataloging-in-Publication Data

Aiken, Lewis R., 1931–
Psychological testing and assessment.

Bibliography: p.
Includes index.
1. Psychological tests. I. Title.
BF176.A48 1988 153.9 87–1287
ISBN 0–205–10623–4

Series Editor: John-Paul Lenney
Senior Editorial Assistant: Leslie Galton
Cover Administrator: Linda Dickinson
Editorial-Production Service: Bywater Production Services

Printed in the United States of America

10 9 8 7 6 5 4 3 2 1 92 91 90 89 88 87

Whatever exists at all exists in some amount. Thorndike, 1918

Anything that exists in amount can be measured. McCall, 1939

Contents

Preface

During the past three decades there has been much criticism of psychological testing and assessment, from psychologists and from other professionals as well. The use of standardized tests in public schools and employment situations, in particular, has been repeatedly attacked for many years. There have been congressional hearings and numerous court cases concerned with testing, and in some states legislation pertaining to test standards and usage has been adopted. Fortunately, the effects of these events have been mainly constructive, and psychological testing has continued to prosper. Increased public and professional awareness of the utility and limitations of testing has stimulated the desire for greater care in designing and marketing psychological tests and other assessment instruments. The need for more carefully trained administrators and interpreters of test results and the personal and social consequences of testing have also become increasingly apparent. The professional concern that tests be designed and used with sensitivity to their scientific accuracy, in addition to the rights of individuals and the welfare of society as a whole, is reflected in the periodic updating of a manual of standards for the construction and use of tests, prepared by a joint committee of psychologists and educators.[1]

[1]The latest edition of this booklet, *Standards for Educational and Psychological Testing,* was prepared by a committee of the American Educational Research Association, the American Psychological Association, and the National Council on Measurement in Education and published in 1985.

Consistent with these concerns and aspirations, the major objective of this book is to improve the knowledge and understanding of those who construct tests, those who take tests, and those who ponder over the meaning and usefulness of test scores. It is designed primarily as a textbook for college students, but it may also serve as a sourcebook of information and procedures for psychologists, educators, and others concerned with testing. The material in the book is appropriate for a one-semester course at the undergraduate or beginning graduate level. My goal was to be comprehensive without being exhaustive, so instructors who adopt the book will find that they still have an important role to play. Ample opportunity remains for the instructor to serve as a selector, interpreter, and elaborator of the material in the book. Furthermore, the Suggested Readings list at the end of each chapter can supplement the material discussed in the chapter.

Part I (Chapters 1–5) deals with the background and methodology of psychological and educational assessment. Certain elementary statistical concepts and formulas required for a basic understanding of psychological measurement are introduced in these chapters, but previous exposure to statistics is not assumed. Part II (Chapters 6–10) deals with the assessment of mental abilities and Part III (Chapters 11–13) with the assessment of personality, interests, and other affective characteristics. Fairly complete descriptions of representative tests and other psychometric instruments in each category are given in Chapters 6–7 and 10–13.

Chapters 8 and 9, which consider research and theories concerned with mental abilities, Chapter 14, which provides an extensive discussion of controversies and issues in testing, and Chapter 15 on the impact of computers and other current developments in psychological assessment are more comprehensive treatments of these topics than usually included in a basic textbook on testing. So too, perhaps, is the discussion of personality theories and research in Chapter 12. I believe, however, that the material in these chapters adds interest and a contextual framework for understanding and evaluating the development and application of psychological assessment instruments. Some of the material presented in these five chapters, and other chapters as well, is controversial, but I have attempted to be objective and fair in discussing the issues, theories, and research findings.

Although this sixth edition of the text consists of fifteen chapters instead of the thirteen chapters of the preceding edition, the book has not been lengthened to an appreciable extent; however, the material has been rewritten, updated, and supplemented wherever it seemed necessary or desirable. Appendixes A and D, the References, and the Test Index should prove helpful in reviewing and locating information on specific tests and procedures. The glossary in Appendix D is fairly detailed, and the separate Author, Subject, and Test indexes should facilitate using the book as either a text or a reference source. The Exercises at the end of each chapter provide relevant practice tasks and thought questions; answers to the quantitative questions are given in Appendix C.

I owe a debt of gratitude to the many students and colleagues who worked their way through the five previous editions of this text and provided valuable comments. Particularly helpful in correcting my spelling and catching my typos in the initial draft of the current edition was Amy Hibbs. I am also grateful to the reviewers of this edition, namely Philip Vernon, University of Western Ontario; Judy Lesiak, Central Michigan University; and Walt Voigt, California Institute of Integral Studies. Finally, Pam Motley and Judith Gimple should be thanked for their untiring efforts to make this edition the best one so far. I sincerely hope that the results of their labors and mine are rewarded by the finished product.

Part I

Methodology of Assessment

Chapter 1

Foundations of Psychological Measurement

Anyone who attends school or college, serves in the armed forces, or applies for a job in the United States usually takes one or more psychological or educational tests. Testing has come to have an important influence on the lives and careers of Americans, as well as people in many other nations. Whenever information is needed to help make decisions about individuals or to assist them in choosing courses of action pertaining to their future educational or occupational status, some form of test may be administered. Tests are used extensively in schools, psychological clinics, industry, and government for the counseling, selection, and placement of people. Considering the many functions of testing, it is not surprising that psychological measurement has become a big business. Professional organizations such as those listed in Appendix A specialize in publishing and distributing psychological tests and other assessment instruments.

HISTORICAL PERSPECTIVE

The fact that people differ in abilities, personality, and behavior and that these differences can be assessed in some way has probably been recognized since the dawn of recorded history. Plato and Aristotle wrote about individual differences, but even they were preempted by the Mandarins of ancient China. As early as 2200 B.C., a civil-service system was instituted by the Chinese emperor to determine if his officials were fit to perform their governmental duties. This system, according to which officials were examined every three years, was continued by later Chinese emperors. Many centuries later, British and French officials in the 1900s patterned their civil-service examination procedures after the ancient Chinese system (DuBois, 1970).

Interest in individual differences, at least from a scientific point of view, was almost nonexistent in Europe during the Middle Ages. In the social structure of medieval European society, a person's activities were dictated by the class into which he or she was born, providing little freedom for personal expression or development. By the sixteenth century, however, European society had become more capitalistic and less doctrinaire; the idea was growing that people are unique and are responsible for asserting their natural gifts and improving their situations. Thus, the Renaissance can be viewed not only as a period during which interest in learning was reawakened but also as a rebirth of individualism. The spirit of individualism, which flourished with the political and economic stimulation provided by capitalism and democracy, found expression in art, science, and government. It was not until the nineteenth century, however, that the scientific study of individual differences actually got underway.

Mental Measurement in the Nineteenth Century

Early in the nineteenth century, scientists generally viewed individual differences in sensorimotor and mental abilities as more of a nuisance than anything else. Before the invention of precise, automatic equipment for measuring and recording physical events, the accuracy of scientific measurements of time, distance, and other physical variables depended to a large extent on the perceptual abilities of human observers. These observers were usually highly trained and very careful in making such measurements, but the measurements made by different people and by the same person on different occasions still varied. Since the search for general laws of nature is difficult when measurements are unreliable, physical scientists directed their attention to the construction of instruments that would be more consistent and precise than unaided human observations.

Stimulated by the writings of Charles Darwin on the origin of species and by the emergence of scientific psychology, interest in the study of individual differences grew during the latter half of the nineteenth century. Darwin, of course, was an Englishman, but scientific psychology was actually inaugurated in Germany during the last quarter of the century. It was during that time that Gustav Fechner, Wilhelm Wundt, Hermann Ebbinghaus, and other German experimental psychologists demonstrated that psychological phenomena could be expressed in quantitative, rational terms. Occurrences in France and the United States were also important to psychological testing. The research of French psychiatrists and psychologists on mental disorders influenced the development of clinical assessment techniques and tests, and the increased attention given to written examinations in American schools resulted in the development of standardized achievement tests and scales.

As is true of the history of any field, many people in several countries played significant roles in the pioneer phase of mental measurement. Especially important during the late 1800s were Sir Francis Galton, James M. Cattell, and Alfred Binet. Galton, a highly gifted cousin of Charles Darwin, was an English gentleman who became interested in the hereditary basis of intelligence and in techniques for measuring abilities. A particular concern of his was the inheritance of genius, but he also devised a number of simple sensorimotor tests and introduced several methods for the investigation of individual differences. Using his simple tests, Galton collected measurements on over 9,000 people ranging in age from 5 to 80. Among his many methodological contributions was the technique of "co-relations," which has continued to be a popular procedure for analyzing test scores.

James M. Cattell was an American who, on returning from Germany after taking his Ph.D. in psychology under Wundt, stopped over in England and became acquainted with Galton's methods and tests while serving as his assistant. Later, at the University of Pennsylvania, Cattell tried relating scores on these simple *mental tests* of reaction time and sensory discrimination to school marks. The "co-relations," however, were very low, and it remained for the Frenchman Alfred Binet to construct the first mental test that proved to be an effective predictor of scholastic achievement.

Testing in the Early Twentieth Century

The psychologist Alfred Binet (Figure 1–1) and his physician-associate Théodore Simon were commissioned in 1904 by the Parisian minister of public instruction to develop a method for identifying children who could not profit sufficiently from instruction in regular school classes. For this purpose Binet and Simon constructed an individually administered test consisting of 30 problems arranged in order of ascending difficulty. The problems on this first workable *intelligence test,* which was published in 1905, emphasized the ability to judge, understand, and reason. A revision of the test, containing a larger number of subtests grouped at age levels from 3 to 13 years, was published in 1908. It was the 1908 revision of the Binet-Simon Intelligence Scale that introduced the concept of *mental age* as a way of expressing an examinee's score on the test. A further revision of the Binet-Simon scale, published in 1911 after Binet's untimely death, extended the test to the adult level.

There were many other pioneers in testing: Charles Spearman in test theory, Edward L. Thorndike in achievement testing, Lewis Terman in intelligence testing, Robert S. Woodworth and Hermann Rorschach in personality testing, and Edward K. Strong in interest measurement, to name a few. The work of Arthur Otis on paper-and-pencil intelligence tests led directly to the construction of the Army Alpha and Army Beta by a committee of psychologists during World War I. These two tests, the Army Alpha for literates and the Army Beta for illiterates, were administered on a group basis to measure the mental abilities of thousands of American soldiers during and after the war.

From World War I to the present, there have been many contributors to

FIGURE 1–1 Alfred Binet.
(Reproduced by permission of Culver Pictures Inc.)

the theory and practice of psychological and educational testing, a number of whom are referred to in Table 1–1. The names of these pioneers are still to be found in the titles of tests and in references to techniques, procedures, and other developments to which they contributed. Among these developments are improvements in statistical methodology, as well as technological advances in the preparation and scoring of tests and the analysis of test results.

TESTING AS A PROFESSION

The field of psychological testing has grown rapidly since the 1920s, and hundreds of tests are now commercially produced and distributed. Many unpublished test materials, cited in professional journals and books, are also available to students and researchers.

Sources of Information

Information concerning psychological tests and other assessment techniques may be obtained from the catalogs of companies that distribute tests (see Appendix A) or, in more detail, from the manuals accompanying the tests themselves. Many reference books dealing with tests are also available. *Tests in Print*

TABLE 1–1 Selected Events in the History of Psychological and Educational Measurement

Date	Event
2200 B.C.	Mandarins set up civil-service testing program in China.
1219 A.D.	First formal oral examinations in law held at University of Bologna.
1575	J. Huarte publishes book, *Examen de Ingenios,* concerned with individual differences in mental abilities.
1636	Oral examinations for degree certification used at Oxford University.
1795	Astronomer Maskelyne of Greenwich Observatory fires his assistant Kinnebrook when their observations of the transit time of Venus disagree.
1860s	Beginning of use of written examinations in schools and governmental organizations in Great Britain, continental Europe, and the U.S.
1869	Scientific study of individual differences begins with publication of Galton's "Classification of Men According to Their Natural Gifts."
1879	Founding of first psychological laboratory in the world by Wilhelm Wundt at Leipzig, Germany.
1884	F. Galton opens Anthropometric Laboratory in London for International Health Exhibition.
1887	G. Fechner formulates the first psychological law.
1888	J. M. Cattell opens testing laboratory at the University of Pennsylvania.
1893	J. Jastrow displays sensorimotor tests at Columbian Exhibition in Chicago.
1897	J. Rice publishes research findings on spelling abilities of U.S. schoolchildren.
1904	C. Spearman describes his two-factor theory of mental abilities.
1905	First Binet-Simon Intelligence Scale published. C. Jung uses word-association test for analysis of mental complexes.
1908	Revision of Binet-Simon Intelligence Scale and C. Stone's Arithmetic Tests published.
1908–14	E. L. Thorndike develops standardized tests of arithmetic, handwriting, language, and spelling.
1916	Stanford-Binet Intelligence Scale published by L. Terman.
1917	Army Alpha and Army Beta, first group intelligence tests, constructed and administered to U.S. army recruits; R. Woodworth's Personal Data Sheet, the first standardized personality inventory, used in military selection.
1919	L. Thurstone's Psychological Examination for College Freshmen published.

TABLE 1–1 *Continued*

1920	National Intelligence Scale published. H. Rorschach's Inkblot Test first published.
1921	Psychological Corporation, first major test publishing company, founded by Cattell, Thorndike, and Woodworth.
1923	First achievement test battery, Stanford Achievement Tests, published.
1924	T. L. Kelley's *Statistical Method* published.
1925–50	Spread of standardized testing, development of methodology and technology of testing.
1927	First edition of Strong Vocational Interest Blank for Men published.
1936	Soviet Union bans psychological tests. First volume of *Psychometrika* published.
1937	Revision of Stanford-Binet Intelligence Scale published.
1938	H. Murray publishes *Explorations in Personality;* O. K. Buros publishes first *Mental Measurements Yearbook.*
1939	Wechsler-Bellevue Intelligence Scale published.
1942	Minnesota Multiphasic Personality Inventory published.
1949	Wechsler Intelligence Scale for Children published.
1960	Form L-M of Stanford-Binet Intelligence Scale published.
1969	A. Jensen's paper on racial inheritance of IQ published in *Harvard Educational Review.*
1970–	Increasing use of computers in designing, administering, scoring, analyzing, and interpreting tests.
1971	Federal court decision requiring tests used in personnel selection to be job relevant *(Griggs* v. *Duke Power).*
1974	Wechsler Intelligence Scale for Children–Revised published.
1975–	Growth of behavioral assessment techniques.
1981	Wechsler Adult Intelligence Scale–Revised published.
1985	*Ninth Mental Measurements Yearbook* published. *Standards for Educational and Psychological Testing* published.

III (Mitchell, 1983), for example, contains descriptive information on 2,674 commercially published tests. Also important are the eight editions of *The Mental Measurements Yearbook* (Buros, 1978 and earlier; Mitchell, 1985), a series of books that describe and review tests. Useful information on tests in specific areas (personality, reading, intelligence, English, foreign languages, mathematics, science, social studies, vocations) may be obtained from the monographs prepared by O. K. Buros and published by Gryphon Press (now available from the University of Nebraska Press). These nine monographs consist of appropriate sections from the seven editions of the *Mental Measurements Yearbook* published from 1938 to 1972 and *Tests in Print II.*

Other books of information on tests are *Tests and Measurements in Child Development: Handbook II* (Johnson, 1976), *Measures for Psychological Assessment* (Chun, Cobb & French, 1976), *Measuring Human Behavior* (Lake, Miles & Earle, 1973), *Tests on Microfiche* (Educational Testing Service), *Directory of Published Experimental Mental Measures* (Vols. 1–4) (Goldman & Busch, 1978, 1982; Goldman & Osborn, 1985; Goldman & Saunders, 1974), *Tests 2d edition* (Sweetland & Keyser, 1986), *Testing Children* (Weaver, 1984), *Testing Adolescents* (Harrington, 1986) and *Testing Adults* (Swiercinsky, 1985). Reviews of selected tests are published in a number of professional journals, for example, *American Educational Research Journal, Measurement and Evaluation in Guidance,* and *Personnel Psychology.*

Articles on the development and evaluation of psychological tests and measures are included in such journals as *Applied Psychological Measurement, Journal of Clinical Psychology, Journal of Clinical and Counseling Psychology, Journal of Counseling Psychology,* and *Journal of Vocational Behavior.* References to sources of information on specific tests are also found in *Psychological Abstracts, Education Index,* and *Current Index to Journal in Education. News on Tests,* a monthly publication of Educational Testing Service, contains announcements of recent published and unpublished tests and citations of test reviews. Educational Testing Service also publishes annotated *Bibliographies* of tests. These detailed descriptions of tests listed under specific categories give the title, author, publication date, target population, publication source, purpose of the test, and the subscores or variables measured.

Standards for Tests

A concern of certain professional organizations of psychologists and educational researchers is that commercially available tests be useful and that they measure what the test authors, publishers, and distributors claim. Representatives of three professional organizations—the American Educational Research Association, the American Psychological Association, and the National Council on Measurement in Education—periodically revise a booklet of technical standards concerning tests, now known as the *Standards for Educational and Psychological Testing* (American Educational Research Association et al., 1985). Test authors, publishers, and consumers are advised to become familiar with these *Standards,* which will be referred to in various contexts throughout this book.

In addition to standards for test development, there are recommended professional standards and qualifications for test users. The qualifications for administering, scoring, and interpreting tests are not uniform. They vary with the particular type of test, being more stringent for individually administered tests of intelligence and personality than for group-administered tests of achievement and special abilities. Whatever the user qualifications may be, the ethical responsibility for ensuring that tests are sold only to qualified persons rests on the shoulders of test publishers and distributors.

Classification of Tests

As is true of any other field, psychological testing and assessment has its own special vocabulary. The glossary in Appendix D provides definitions of the most frequently used measurement terms, many of which refer to types of tests or methods of classifying tests. One such method of classification is the dichotomy *standardized versus nonstandardized.* The standardized test item is considered to be one of the most important contributions of modern psychology (Jackson, 1974). A *standardized test* is simply one that has fixed directions for administration and scoring, having been constructed by professional test makers and administered to a representative sample of examinees from the population for whom the test is intended. Various types of converted scores, or *norms,* may be computed from the raw test scores of this sample group (the standardization group) of examinees; these norms serve as a basis for interpreting the scores of subsequent examinees. Even more common than published standardized tests are nonstandardized classroom tests, which are usually constructed by a teacher in an informal manner for a single administration.

Tests are also classified as *individual* or *group.* An *individual test,* like the Binet-Simon Intelligence Scale, is administered to one examinee at a time. A *group test,* such as the Army Examination Alpha, can be administered to many examinees simultaneously.

Whereas the dichotomy *individual versus group* is related to the efficiency of administration, *speed versus power* pertains to the time limits of a test. A pure *speed test* consists of many easy items, but the time limits are very stringent, and almost no one finishes in the time allotted. In contrast, time limits on a *power test* are generous, but the test contains many difficult items.

A third classification dichotomy, *objective versus nonobjective,* is concerned with the method of scoring. An *objective test* has fixed, objective scoring standards, and can be scored by a clerk. On the other hand, the scoring of essay tests and certain types of personality tests is often quite subjective, and two scorers may obtain different results.

Tests may also be classified according to content, or the task that they pose for an examinee. Some tests contain only *verbal* materials (e.g., vocabulary and sentences), whereas others consist of *nonverbal* materials (e.g., diagrams and puzzles). A test may also require that the examinee manipulate objects—for example, putting pegs into holes. That kind of test is called a *performance test.*

Another broad classification of tests according to content or process is *cognitive versus affective. Cognitive tests* measure the processes and products of mental ability (cognition) and frequently are subclassified as tests of achievement and aptitude. An *achievement test,* which assesses knowledge of some school subject or occupation, focuses on the examinee's past behavior (what has already been learned or accomplished). An *aptitude test* focuses on future behavior, that is, what a person is capable of learning with appropriate training. Thus, tests of mechanical aptitude and clerical aptitude are designed to assess the ability to profit from further training in mechanical and clerical tasks, respectively. Achievement and aptitude however are not separate entities; what a person has accomplished in the past is usually a fairly good indicator of what can be expected in the future. In fact, some psychologists prefer not to use the terms *achievement* and *aptitude* at all as ways of classifying tests, referring to both kinds of tests as measures of ability.

Affective tests are designed to assess interests, attitudes, values, motives, temperament traits, and other noncognitive aspects of personality. A variety of techniques—behavioral observation, paper-and-pencil inventories, and projective pictures—have been designed for this purpose.

Certain institutions and organizations that maintain collections of psychological and educational tests have formal systems for classifying these instruments. One of the most comprehensive classification systems is that of *The Mental Measurements Yearbook.* In this system, the major headings of which are reproduced in Table 1–2, tests are classified into sixteen broad content categories. Because 1,409 different tests are listed in the ninth edition of the yearbook, the need for a fairly detailed classification system is obvious.

Frequency of Test Usage

Accurate information on the frequency of usage of various tests is difficult to obtain, but there have been a few surveys. Brown and McGuire (1976) asked representatives of 249 community mental health agencies and hospitals throughout the United States how frequently they administered each of twenty-nine

TABLE 1–2

Major Categories and Corresponding Percentages of Tests Listed in *The Ninth Mental Measurements Yearbook*

Category of test	*Percentage of total*	*Rank*
Achievement Batteries	4.83	7
Fine Arts	.64	14
Intelligence and Scholastic Aptitude	7.10	5
Languages	9.51	4
Mathematics	3.26	9
Miscellaneous	9.87	3
Motor/Visual Motor	1.63	12
Multi-Aptitude	.57	15
Neuropsychological	.99	13
Personality	24.84	1
Reading	6.88	6
Science	1.85	11
Social Studies	.35	16
Speech and Hearing	2.77	10
Vocations	20.94	2
Developmental	3.97	8

Source: Adapted from *The Ninth Mental Measurements Yearbook* by permission of The Buros Institute of Mental Measurements of the University of Nebraska–Lincoln. Copyright 1985.

selected tests. Compared with the findings of a similar survey conducted by Sundberg (1961) some years earlier, it was found that the Wechsler Intelligence Scales became more popular while the Stanford-Binet Intelligence Scale declined in popularity in the particular settings surveyed. Projectives such as the Rorschach Inkblot Test and the Machover Draw-a-Person Test also fell in the rankings from 1961 to 1976, while the Minnesota Multiphasic Personality Inventory (MMPI)—a more objective personality assessment instrument—rose.

A somewhat different picture of the popularity of certain tests was obtained in a survey of 500 clinical psychologists sampled from members of the Division of Clinical Psychology of the American Psychological Association (Wade & Baker, 1977). Although the results of Brown and McGuire's (1976) survey placed the Rorschach Inkblot and the Thematic Apperception Test in fifth and sixth places, respectively, they were first and second, respectively, in the Wade and Baker (1977) survey.

A more recent survey of the frequency of test usage by professional psychologists (Lubin, Larsen & Matarazzo, 1984) was conducted on a sample of 221 psychologists employed in psychiatric hospitals, community mental health centers and community clinics, schools for the mentally retarded, counseling centers, and Veterans Administration hospitals. The thirty most frequently mentioned instruments, in order of frequency, are listed in Table 1–3. These findings, obtained in 1982, are similar to those of the Brown and McGuire (1976) survey.

Citations in the professional testing literature are another source of information on the popularity of specific tests. The numbers in Table 1–2, for example, are the percentages of tests listed in the corresponding sixteen categories of *The Ninth Mental Measurements Yearbook.* Note that approximately 45 percent of the tests are in the personality and vocations categories; achievement and intelligence tests are also cited frequently. The top ten tests, in terms of the number of times they are cited in *The Ninth Mental Measurements Yearbook,* are listed in Table 1–4.

MEASUREMENT AND STATISTICS

Any kind of physical measurement (of size, weight, coloration, and so forth) made on living things will show variability across individuals. Human beings differ physically from each other in many ways—in height, weight, blood pressure, visual acuity, and so on. Similarly, there are extensive individual differences in mental characteristics and behavior. People differ in abilities, knowledge, interests, attitudes, and temperament, to name a few psychological variables. Some of these individual differences can be measured more precisely than others, depending on the type of measurement scale.

Scales of Measurement

The measurement of physical and psychological variables can be characterized by the degree of refinement or precision in terms of four measurement scales: nominal, ordinal, interval, and ratio. Measurement is on a *nominal scale* when-

TABLE 1–3 Psychological Tests Used Most Frequently by Clinical Psychologists

Test	*Usage rank*
Wechsler Adult Intelligence Scale	1
Minnesota Multiphasic Personality Inventory	2
Bender Visual Motor Gestalt Test	3
Rorschach Inkblot Test	4
Thematic Apperception Test	5
Wechsler Intelligence Scale for Children–Revised	6
Peabody Picture Vocabulary Test	7.5
Sentence Completion Test (all kinds)	7.5
House-Tree-Person Test	9
Draw-a-Person Test	10
Wechsler Memory Scale	11
Rotter Sentence Completion Test	12
Memory for Designs	13
Vineland Social Maturity Scale	14
Stanford-Binet Intelligence Scale	15
Strong Vocational Interest Blank–Men	16
Bender Visual Retention Test	17.5
Edwards Personal Preference Schedule	17.5
Strong Vocational Interest Blank–Women	19
Children's Apperception Test	20.5
Progressive Matrices	20.5
Kuder Preference Record	22
Porteus Mazes	23
Full Range Picture Vocabulary Test	24
Differential Aptitude Tests	25
Gray Oral Reading Test	26
Wechsler-Bellevue Intelligence Scale	27
Cattell Infant Intelligence Test	28
Goldstein-Scheerer Tests of Abstract and Concrete Thinking	29
Blacky Pictures	30

Source: From Lubin, B., Larsen, R.M. & Matarazzo, J.D., 1984. Patterns of psychological test usage in the United States: 1935–1982. *American Psychologist, 39,* 451–454. Copyright 1984 by the American Psychological Association. Adapted by permission of the publisher and authors.

ever numbers are used merely to describe or name rather than to indicate the order or amount of something. An example of nominal measurement is the numbering of basketball uniforms or categories of people. These numbers are used only to designate individuals or groups; it makes no sense to compare them in terms of magnitude. Somewhat more refined than nominal measurement is an *ordinal scale.* On this type of measurement scale, the numbers refer to the ranks of objects or events on some order of merit. For example, numbers designating the order of finishing in a race or other contest are on an ordinal

TABLE 1–4 Reference Frequencies and Ranks for the Ten Tests Cited Most Often in *The Ninth Mental Measurements Yearbook*

Test	*Number of references*	*Rank*
Minnesota Multiphasic Personality Inventory	339	1
Wechsler Intelligence Scale for Children–Revised	299	2
Wechsler Adult Intelligence Scale–Revised	291	3
State-Trait Anxiety Inventory	158	4
Bem Sex-Role Inventory	121	5
Peabody Picture Vocabulary Test–Revised	117	6
Wide Range Achievement Test, 1978 Edition	103	7
Eysenck Personality Inventory	91	8
Halstead-Reitan Neuropsychological Test Battery	79	9.5
Rorschach Inkblot Test	79	9.5

Source: Reprinted from *The Ninth Mental Measurements Yearbook* by permission of The Buros Institute of Mental Measurements at The University of Nebraska–Lincoln. Copyright 1985.

scale. A third level of measurement is an *interval scale,* on which equal numerical differences can be interpreted as being equal differences in whatever characteristic is being measured. The Celsius scale of temperature is a good illustration of an equal-interval scale. For example, the difference between 60°C and 40°C is equal to the difference between 30°C and 10°C, both numerically and in terms of temperature (heat). The standard score scale of intelligence (see Chapters 4 and 7) is also considered to be an equal-interval scale.

The highest or most refined level of measurement is a *ratio scale,* a scale of measurement having the characteristics of an interval scale in addition to a true zero—a point signifying the complete absence of whatever is being measured. When measurement is on a ratio scale, numerical ratios can be interpreted in a meaningful way. For example, the variable of height is measured on a ratio scale. Therefore, if John is 72 inches tall and Paul is 36 inches tall, one can correctly state that John is twice as tall as Paul. Height, weight, energy, and many other physical variables are measured on ratio scales, but psychological characteristics are not. The scores on psychological tests represent ordinal, or at most interval, measurement rather than ratio measurement. For this reason, even if Frank's IQ score is 150 and Jim's IQ is 100, it is incorrect to conclude that Jim is two-thirds as intelligent as Frank. Furthermore, if IQs represent only ordinal numbers and Amy has an IQ of 50, then it would be incorrect to state that the difference in intelligence between Jim and Frank (150 − 100) is equal to the difference in intelligence between Frank and Amy (100 − 50).

Frequency Distributions

The range and distribution of individual differences in physical and mental characteristics may be depicted by means of a frequency distribution of scores on a test or some other measuring device. In its simplest form, a *frequency distribution* is a list of possible scores and the number of examinees who make each score. For example, if a five-item test is administered and an examinee gets one point for each item answered correctly, the possible scores are 0, 1, 2, 3, 4, and 5. If the test is administered to twenty-five examinees, a frequency distribution of their scores might look like this:

Score	0	1	2	3	4	5
Number of examinees (frequency)	2	3	6	9	4	1

From this frequency distribution, it may be observed that two examinees missed all five items, nine examinees answered three items correctly, and one examinee answered all five items correctly.

Score Intervals When the range of scores on a test is large, say 25 points or more, it is usually more convenient to group the scores into intervals. To illustrate, intelligence quotient (IQ) scores on the Wechsler Adult Intelligence Scale (WAIS) range from approximately 43 to 152. Computations made on these scores may be simplified by grouping them into intervals of five IQ points, starting with the interval 43–47, and counting up through the interval 148–152 (see column 1 of Table 1–5). This gives 22 intervals instead of the 110 (IQs from 43 through 152) that would result if an interval were allotted to every possible score. Using the smaller number of intervals will have very little effect on the accuracy of the statistics to be computed from the test scores.

Histogram and Frequency Polygon A useful pictorial way of representing a frequency distribution of scores is to graph the distribution as a histogram or frequency polygon. To begin the construction of a histogram, the exact limits of the score intervals must be determined. The *exact limits* of an interval are computed by subtracting 0.5 from the lower limit and adding 0.5 to the upper limit of the interval. For example, the exact limits of the interval 43–47 are 42.5–47.5, and the exact limits of the interval 148–152 are 147.5–152.5. After the exact limits have been found, the frequency corresponding to each interval is represented as a vertical bar with a width spanning the exact limits and a height proportional to the interval frequency. A completed histogram of the frequency distribution in Table 1–5 is represented by the adjacent vertical bars in Figure 1–2.

In order for the graphical plot of a frequency distribution to have a curved appearance, the data are often plotted as a series of connected line segments. In Figure 1–2, the dashed line segments connecting the midpoints of the score intervals form a frequency polygon of the distribution in Table 1–5. Viewed

TABLE 1–5 Frequency Distribution of Full Scale IQs on Wechsler Adult Intelligence Scale (N = 2,052)

(1) *IQ interval*	*(2)* *Number of examinees (frequency)*
148–152	1
143–147	0
138–142	3
133–137	12
128–132	26
123–127	64
118–122	145
113–117	165
108–112	224
103–107	274
98–102	278
93–97	255
88–92	220
83–87	135
78–82	107
73–77	55
68–72	49
63–67	18
58–62	11
53–57	6
48–52	3
43–47	1

Source: Data from D. Wechsler, *The measurement and appraisal of adult intelligence* (4th ed.). Baltimore: Williams & Wilkins, 1958, p. 253. © 1958 The Williams & Wilkins Co., Baltimore. Reproduced by permission of Oxford University Press.

alone, the frequency polygon gives a better picture of the overall shape of the frequency distribution than the histogram does.

The Normal Curve Although the frequency polygon in Figure 1–2 looks irregular, it approaches a symmetrical, bell-shaped form. More examinees made scores of approximately 100 (actually 98–102) than any other score, and fewer and fewer examinees made scores increasingly lower or increasingly higher than 100. If the frequency polygon were perfectly symmetrical, smooth, and bell-shaped, it would look like the drawing in Figure 1–3.

The curve in Figure 1–3, which can be described by a mathematical equation, is a *normal curve.* The scores on the base axis of this figure are *standard scores (z scores).* These z scores, the computation of which is described in Chapter 4, serve as a convenient, standard method of expressing and comparing scores.

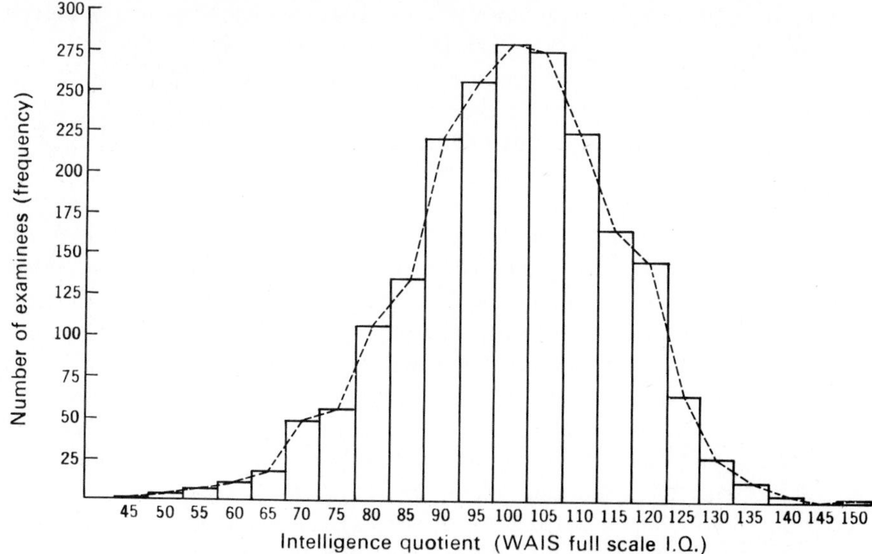

Histogram and Frequency Polygon of Frequency Distribution in Table 1–5. **FIGURE 1–2**
(Wechsler, D. *The measurement and appraisal of adult intelligence* [4th ed.]. Baltimore: Williams & Wilkins, 1958, p. 253. © 1958 The Williams & Wilkins Co., Baltimore. Reproduced by permission of Oxford University Press.)

A certain percentage of the area under the curve in Figure 1–3 lies between any two z scores. This percentage may correspond to the percentage of a group of examinees whose raw test scores, when converted to z scores, fall within the range of the two z scores. For example, 19.15 percent of the area under the curve in Figure 1–3, and consequently 19.15 percent of a normal distribution of test scores, falls between z scores of 0 and 0.5. Only 1.66 percent of the area under the normal curve, however, lies between $z = +2.0$ and $z = +2.5$ (or -2.0 and -2.5).

Although the theoretical range of z scores in a normal distribution is minus infinity ($-\infty$) to plus infinity ($+\infty$), over 99 percent of the area under the

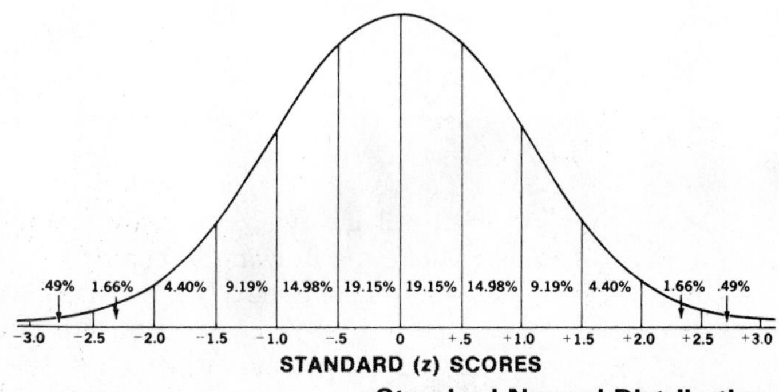

Standard Normal Distribution. **FIGURE 1–3**

normal curve (or 99 percent of a normal distribution of test scores) falls between z scores of -3.00 and $+3.00$. Of course, when converting a raw test score to a z score, the result is not always one of the thirteen z scores listed on the base axis of Figure 1–3. Therefore, a special table, from which the reader can determine the percentage of the area falling below any z score, must be provided (see Appendix B).

During the late nineteenth and early twentieth centuries there was much speculation concerning the normal curve as a "law of nature," since the frequency distributions of so many biological characteristics seem to be approximately normal in shape. In fact, much of the mathematical theory of statistical inference, which is so important in psychological and educational research, is based on the assumption of a normal distribution of measurements. The reader should be cautioned, however, not to glorify the normal curve. Although many tests are constructed in such a way that the scores are approximately normally distributed, the frequency distributions of other test scores are quite asymmetrical, or skewed. A common situation is a *positively skewed* distribution of scores (few high scores and many low scores), the consequence of a test that is too difficult for the examinees. Less common is a *negatively skewed* score distribution (many high scores and few low scores), which occurs when a test is too easy for the examinees (Figure 1–4).

Averages

In addition to knowing how to describe the way in which a group of test scores are distributed, it is convenient to have some measure of the average score. Three types of averages will be discussed: the mode, the median, and the arithmetic mean.

Mode The *mode* of a set of test scores is usually defined as the score obtained by the largest number of examinees. In the five-item test referred to previously, the mode is 3, because more people (9) made that score than any other. When test scores are grouped into intervals, the mode is defined as the midpoint of

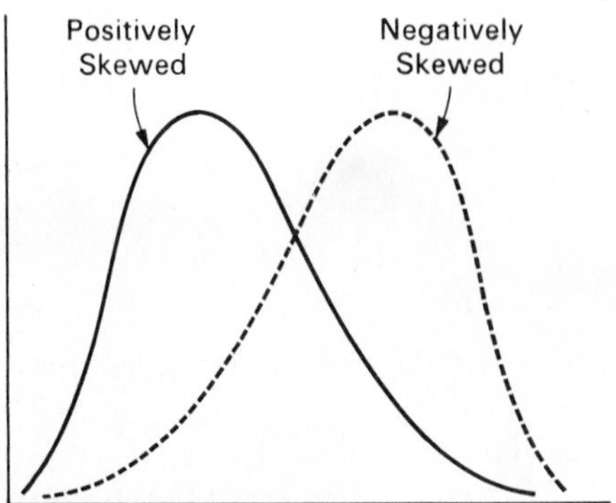

FIGURE 1–4 Skewed Frequency Distributions.

the interval containing the largest number of scores. In Table 1–5, the score interval 98–102 contains the largest number of scores (278). The midpoint of that interval is 100, computed as

$$X'_M = \frac{98 + 102}{2} = 100,$$

so 100 is the mode of this frequency distribution of scores. As illustrated in the frequency polygon (Figure 1–2), the mode may also be viewed as the maximum point in a frequency distribution. Sometimes there is more than one maximum point in a distribution of scores, in which case the distribution is said to be *bimodal* if it has two maxima and *multimodal* if it has more than two.

Median The *median* (Mdn) of a group of scores is the middle score, or that score below and above which one-half (50 percent) of the scores fall. Thus, the median of the group of scores 7, 6, 9, 5, and 3 is 6, because 6 is in the middle when the scores are ranked from highest to lowest.

Computing the median of a frequency distribution of scores is more involved, but it can be determined rather quickly by finding the interval within which the median lies and interpolating within that interval. To illustrate the procedure, the median of the frequency distribution in Table 1–5 will be determined. Since the total number of scores is 2,052, the median is the score (IQ) below and above which .50(2,052) = 1,026 of the scores fall. By successively adding the frequencies in column 2 of Table 1–5, it is determined that there are 860 scores up through an IQ score of 97 and 1,138 scores up through an IQ score of 102. In order to make the distribution of scores continuous, the exact upper limits of the score intervals in the frequency distribution are calculated. In the distribution of Table 1–5, there are 860 scores up through an upper limit of 97.5 and 1,138 scores up through an upper limit of 102.5. Since the median is the score below which 1,026 scores fall, it must lie between 97.5 and 102.5. To find the exact median of these data, we form the ratio

$$\frac{\text{Mdn} - 97.5}{102.5 - 97.5} = \frac{1026 - 860}{1138 - 860},$$

which reduces to

$$\frac{\text{Mdn} - 97.5}{5} = \frac{166}{278}.$$

Solving the last equation for the median gives

$$\text{Mdn} = 97.5 + 5\left(\frac{166}{278}\right) = 100.49.$$

The procedure described for finding the median may be expressed more formally by the following equation:

$$\text{Mdn} = L + w\left(\frac{.5n_t - n_l}{n_i}\right), \qquad (1.1)$$

where L is the lower exact limit of the interval containing the median, w the width of the interval containing the median, n_t the total number of scores in the distribution, n_l the total number of scores falling below the interval containing the median, and n_i the number of scores within the interval containing the median.

The Summation Operator Before studying the methods of computing the arithmetic mean, the reader needs to become familiar with the special symbol Σ. Σ (sigma) is used in statistics as a shorthand way of referring to the arithmetic operation of adding a series of values that a variable may assume. Thus,

$$\sum_{i=1}^{n} X_i$$

means "the sum of all values of the variable X_i, where i is an index number ranging from 1 to $n(i = 1, 2, 3, \ldots, n)$." In symbols,

$$\sum_{i=1}^{n} X_i = X_1 + X_2 + X_3 \cdots + X_n.$$

To illustrate, let $n = 3, X_1 = 2, X_2 = 4$, and $X_3 = 1$; then, since $i = 1, 2$, and 3 in this case,

$$\sum_{i=1}^{3} X_i = 2 + 4 + 1 = 7.$$

Similarly,

$$\sum_{i=1}^{3} X_i^2 = (X_1)^2 + (X_2)^2 + (X_3)^2$$
$$= (2)^2 + (4)^2 + (1)^2 = 4 + 16 + 1 = 21.$$

The usefulness of the summation operation (Σ) becomes apparent when two or more variables are involved. For example,

$$\sum_{i=1}^{n} (X_i + Y_i) = \sum_{i=1}^{n} X_i + \sum_{i=1}^{n} Y_i;$$

so if $Y_1 = 3, Y_2 = 5$, and $Y_3 = 2$, and the values of X_i are those given above,

$$\sum_{i=1}^{3}(X_i + Y_i) = (X_1 + Y_1) + (X_2 + Y_2) + (X_3 + Y_3)$$
$$= (2 + 3) + (4 + 5) + (1 + 2) = 17.$$

The same result can be obtained as

$$\sum_{i=1}^{3} X_i + \sum_{i=1}^{3} Y_i = (2 + 4 + 1) + (3 + 5 + 2) = 7 + 10 = 17.$$

Also, for the same data, the sum of the products of X and Y is computed as

$$\sum_{i=1}^{3} X_iY_i = (X_1Y_1) + (X_2Y_2) + (X_3Y_3) = 2(3) + 4(5) + 1(2)$$
$$= 6 + 20 + 2 = 28.$$

Two rules for the use of constants in conjunction with the summation operator are:

1. The sum of a constant (c) times a variable equals the constant times the sum of the variable, or

$$\sum_{i=1}^{n} cX_i = c\sum_{i=1}^{n} X_i.$$

2. The sum of a constant equals n times the constant, or

$$\sum_{i=1}^{n} c = nc.$$

Finally, by using the binomial expansion of high school algebra, one can write

$$\sum_{i=1}^{n} (X_i + Y_i)^2 = \sum_{i=1}^{n} X_i^2 + 2\sum_{i=1}^{n} X_iY_i + \sum_{i=1}^{n} Y_i^2.$$

The reader should verify these rules for $c = 5$ and the values of X_i and Y_i given above.

Sometimes, when it is clearly understood that the limits of the summation are 1 and n, the numbers above and below the summation sign and the subscripts on the variables are omitted. For the sake of clarity, however, the limits of the summation and the i (or j) subscript on all variables are always indicated in this book.

Arithmetic Mean Although the mode is an easily computed average, it is greatly affected by the shape of the score distribution. The median is less affected by the shape of the distribution and, in fact, is the preferred average when the distribution is highly asymmetrical, or skewed. However, the arithmetic mean is the most popular measure of the average score because the median is cumbersome to work with from the viewpoint of statistical theory. To compute an arithmetic mean, the scores (X_i) are added, and the resulting sum is divided by the number of scores (n):

$$\bar{X} = \sum_{i=1}^{n} \frac{X_i}{n}. \quad (1.2)$$

When scores are grouped in the form of a frequency distribution the mean can be found more quickly by (1) multiplying the midpoint (X_i') of each score interval by the frequency (f_i) on the interval, (2) adding these products, and (3) dividing the resulting sum of products by the total number of scores (n):

$$\bar{X} = \sum_{i=1}^{g} \frac{f_iX_i'}{n}, \quad (1.3)$$

where g is the number of intervals (groups). To illustrate, in the five-item problem described earlier, the arithmetic mean is

$$\overline{X} = \frac{2(0) + 3(1) + 6(2) + 9(3) + 4(4) + 1(5)}{25} = \frac{63}{25} = 2.52.$$

As an exercise, the reader should verify that the mean of the distribution in Table 1–5 is 99.96.

Percentiles, Deciles, and Quartiles

The median is sometimes referred to as the 50th percentile, because 50 percent of the scores in a frequency distribution fall below the median. The entire distribution of scores may, of course, be divided into 100 percentiles, the "pth" *percentile* being that score below which p percent of the scores fall. For example, the 25th percentile is the score below which 25 percent of the scores fall, the 40th percentile the score below which 40 percent of the scores fall, and the 75th percentile the score below which 75 percent of the scores fall. Any of these, or any other percentile, can be computed by the same procedure as that described for finding the median.

In addition to percentiles, a distribution of scores may be divided into tenths *(deciles)* or fourths *(quartiles)*. For example, the fourth decile (or 40th percentile) is the score below which four-tenths of the scores fall, and the third quartile (75th percentile) is the score below which three-fourths of the scores fall. Note that the 50th percentile, the fifth decile, and the second quartile are all the same score—the median.

Variability

A measure of the average or central tendency such as the arithmetic mean, the median, or the mode is not sufficient by itself to describe a group of test scores. Different groups of scores differ not only in their averages but also in their degree of spread or *variability*. Three measures of variability are the range, the semi-interquartile range, and the standard deviation.

Range and Semi-interquartile Range The simple *range,* defined as the highest minus the lowest score, is the easiest measure of variability to compute. As an illustration, the range of the data in the five-item problem is $5 - 0 = 5$, and the range of the IQ scores in Table 1–5 is $152 - 43 = 109$. Because it is markedly affected by a single very high or very low score, the range is a poor measure of variability in most instances. A modified type of range known as the *semi-interquartile range* is sometimes used as an index of variability when the distribution of test scores is greatly skewed. The semi-interquartile range, or Q, is computed as one-half the difference between the 75th percentile (third quartile) and the 25th percentile (first quartile).

As an exercise, the reader may wish to verify that, for the frequency distribution in Table 1–5, the first quartile is 90.41, the third quartile 110.33, and the semi-interquartile range 9.96. The two quartiles may be found by the linear interpolation method that was used earlier in the chapter. Because the first quartile is that score below which .25(2,052) = 513 scores fall, we must interpolate within the score interval 87.5 – 92.5; to find the third quartile, or .75(2,052) = 1,539th score, we interpolate within the interval 107.5 – 112.5.

Standard Deviation The most common measure of variability, the *standard deviation,* is appropriate when the arithmetic mean is the reported average. To compute the standard deviation of a set of raw scores:

1. Subtract the arithmetic mean from each score.
2. Square the differences.
3. Add the squared differences.
4. Divide the sum of the squared differences by 1 less than the number of scores.
5. Extract the square root of the quotient obtained in step 4.

A formula including these five steps is

$$s = \sqrt{\sum_{i=1}^{n} \frac{(X_i - \overline{X})^2}{n - 1}}. \qquad (1.4)$$

As an example, let us compute the standard deviation of the scores 7, 6, 9, 5, and 3. The arithmetic mean of these scores is

$$\overline{X} = \frac{7 + 6 + 9 + 5 + 3}{5} = 6.$$

Subtracting the arithmetic mean from each score gives the differences $(X_i - \overline{X}) = 1, 0, 3, -1$, and -3. The squares of these differences are $(X_i - \overline{X})^2 =$ 1, 0, 9, 1, and 9, respectively, and the sum of the squared differences is

$$\sum_{i=1}^{n} (X_i - \overline{X})^2 = 20.$$

Dividing this total by $n - 1 = 4$, 1 less than the number of scores, yields $20/4 = 5$. This quotient, 5, is the variance (s^2) of the five scores; the square root of the variance, $s = 2.24$, is the standard deviation of the scores.

Standard Deviation of a Frequency Distribution Computing the standard deviation of a frequency distribution is a bit more complicated than using raw scores, but the procedure is similar:

1. Subtract the arithmetic mean from the midpoint of each interval.
2. Square these differences.
3. Multiply the squared differences by the respective interval frequencies.

4. Sum these products.
5. Divide the sum of products by 1 less than the number of scores.
6. Extract the square root of the resulting quotient to give the standard deviation.

The formula is

$$s = \sqrt{\sum_{i=1}^{g} \frac{f_i(X'_i - \overline{X})^2}{n - 1}}. \tag{1.5}$$

To illustrate the computational procedure, the standard deviation of the five-item problem referred to earlier will be determined:

1. Subtracting the arithmetic mean from the midpoint of each interval yields the differences $0 - 2.52 = -2.52$, $1 - 2.52 = -1.52$, $2 - 2.52 = -.52$, $3 - 2.52 = .48$, $4 - 2.52 = 1.48$, and $5 - 2.52 = 2.48$.
2. Squaring these differences yields $(-2.52)^2 = 6.35$, $(-1.52)^2 = 2.31$, $(-.52)^2 = .27$, $(.48)^2 = .23$, $(1.48)^2 = 2.19$, $(2.48)^2 = 6.15$.
3. Multiplying these squares by the respective interval frequencies gives $2(6.35) = 12.70$, $3(2.31) = 6.93$, $6(.27) = 1.62$, $9(.23) = 2.07$, $4(2.19) = 8.76$, $1(6.15) = 6.15$.
4. Adding these products, the sum is $12.70 + 6.93 + 1.62 + 2.07 + 8.76 + 6.15 = 38.23$.
5. Dividing this sum by 1 less than the number of scores yields $38.23/24 = 1.59$.
6. Extracting the square root of 1.59 gives 1.26 as the standard deviation.

To make certain that the procedure for computing the standard deviation of a frequency distribution is understood, the reader should verify that for the distribution in Table 1–5, $s = 14.85$.

Correlation

Francis Galton is credited with the initial work on the method of correlation ("co-relation"). In the field of testing, this method has been employed more than any other procedure for analyzing data, and it is also very important in the statistical theory of mental test scores. The method of correlation is concerned with determining the degree to which two sets of measures, such as intelligence and academic achievement, are related. The degree and direction of relationship between two variables is expressed as a numerical index known as the *correlation coefficient.* Although there are many different types of correlation coefficient, the Pearson *product-moment coefficient,* or r, is the most common. r ranges in value from -1.00 (perfect inverse relationship) through .00 (absence of a relationship) to $+1.00$ (perfect direct relationship).

Computing the Product-Moment Coefficient Table 1–6 illustrates the computations needed to determine the correlation between the scores of thirty examinees on two measures, X and Y. Measure X might be an ability test of some sort and measure Y a criterion of occupational success. Thus, examinee 1 has a score of 44 on measure X and a score of 69 on measure Y, while examinee 2 has an X score of 38 and a Y score of 46. The column headings indicate the steps in computing r:

1. Compute X_i^2, Y_i^2, and the X_iY_i products for each examinee (columns 4, 5, and 6).

TABLE 1–6 Computing Sums for Determining the Correlation between X and Y

(1) Examinee	(2) X_i	(3) Y_i	(4) X_i^2	(5) Y_i^2	(6) X_iY_i
1	44	69	1,936	4,761	3,036
2	38	46	1,444	2,116	1,748
3	56	51	3,136	2,601	2,856
4	54	44	2,916	1,936	2,376
5	66	53	4,356	2,809	3,498
6	52	49	2,704	2,401	2,548
7	46	43	2,116	1,849	1,978
8	36	35	1,296	1,225	1,260
9	44	37	1,936	1,369	1,628
10	60	69	3,600	4,761	4,140
11	22	31	484	961	682
12	72	47	5,184	2,209	3,384
13	56	45	3,136	2,025	2,520
14	52	41	2,704	1,681	2,132
15	50	39	2,500	1,521	1,950
16	64	65	4,096	4,225	4,160
17	40	36	1,600	1,296	1,440
18	28	59	784	3,481	1,652
19	68	70	4,624	4,900	4,760
20	48	53	2,304	2,809	2,544
21	32	51	1,024	2,601	1,632
22	74	63	5,476	3,969	4,662
23	42	54	1,764	2,916	2,268
24	50	52	2,500	2,704	2,600
25	40	49	1,600	2,401	1,960
26	58	48	3,364	2,304	2,784
27	62	60	3,844	3,600	3,720
28	54	64	2,916	4,096	3,456
29	60	55	3,600	3,025	3,300
30	30	33	900	1,089	990
Sums	1,498	1,511	79,844	79,641	77,664

2. Compute the sums of the X_i, Y_i, X_i^2, Y_i^2, and X_iY_i columns $\left(\sum_{i=1}^{n} X_i, \sum_{i=1}^{n} Y_i, \sum_{i=1}^{n} X_i^2, \sum_{i=1}^{n} Y_i^2, \sum_{i=1}^{n} X_iY_i\right)$ and substitute these values in the following formula:

$$r = \frac{n\sum_{i=1}^{n} X_iY_i - \left(\sum_{i=1}^{n} X_i\right)\left(\sum_{i=1}^{n} Y_i\right)}{\sqrt{n\sum_{i=1}^{n} X_i^2 - \left(\sum_{i=1}^{n} X_i\right)^2}\sqrt{n\sum_{i=1}^{n} Y_i^2 - \left(\sum_{i=1}^{n} Y_i\right)^2}} \qquad (1.6)$$

Since

$$\sum_{i=1}^{n} X_i = 1{,}498, \sum_{i=1}^{n} Y_i = 1{,}511, \sum_{i=1}^{n} X_i^2 = 79{,}844, \sum_{i=1}^{n} Y_i^2 = 79{,}641,$$

$$\text{and} \sum_{i=1}^{n} X_iY_i = 77{,}664,$$

$$r = \frac{30(77{,}664) - (1{,}498)(1{,}511)}{\sqrt{30(79{,}844) - (1{,}498)^2}\sqrt{30(79{,}641) - (1{,}511)^2}} = .52.$$

The Meaning of Correlation The method of correlation is useful in the field of testing for a number of reasons, among which is the fact that correlation implies prediction. The accuracy with which an individual's score on measure *Y* can be predicted from his or her score on measure *X* depends on the magnitude of the correlation between the *X* scores and *Y* scores. The closer the correlation coefficient is to an absolute value of 1.00 (either + 1.00 or − 1.00), the smaller the average error in making predictions of scores on *Y* from scores on *X*. For example, if the correlation coefficient between tests *X* and *Y* is close to +1.00, it can be predicted with high confidence that a person who makes a high score on *X* will also score high on *Y* and that a person who scores low on *X* will also score low on *Y*. On the other hand, if the correlation between tests *X* and *Y* is close to −1.00, it can be predicted that a person who scores high on *X* will score low on *Y* and one who scores low on *X* will score high on *Y*. The closer the value of the correlation coefficient is to +1.00 or −1.00, the more accurate these predictions will be; the closer the correlation coefficient is to .00, the less accurate the predictions will be. And when the correlation coefficient is equal to .00, predicting an individual's score on one measure from his or her score on the other measure is no more accurate than random guessing.

Although correlation implies prediction, it does not imply causation. The fact that two variables are related does not mean that either variable is necessarily a cause of the other. Both may be under the influence of a third variable, and the correlation between the first two variables is a reflection of this common cause. To illustrate, it can be demonstrated that mental age in a group of children of various chronological ages has a slight positive correlation with foot size.

Obviously neither mental age nor foot size is a "cause" of the other; the positive correlation between them is due to the effects of a third variable—body growth or maturation. Thus, the fact that variables X and Y are significantly correlated makes the prediction of a Y score from an X score (or an X score from a Y score) more accurate. However, it provides no information on whether X and Y are causally related.

Regression and Prediction The product-moment correlation coefficient, a measure of the *linear* relationship between two variables, is actually a by-product of the statistical procedure for finding the equation of a straight line that best depicts how the two variables are related. In order to illustrate the meaning of this statement, the X, Y pairs of values listed in Table 1–6 have been plotted graphically in Figure 1–5. Clearly, all these points will not fall on any one straight line, but a straight line can be fitted to the points in such a way that the sum of the squared vertical distances of the points from that line will be smaller than for any other straight line. The equation for this best-fitting line is

$$Y_{\text{pred}} = r\frac{s_y}{s_x}(X - \bar{X}) + \bar{Y}, \qquad (1.7)$$

where Y_{pred} is the predicted value of Y, r is the coefficient of correlation between X and Y, s_x and s_y are the standard deviations of X and Y, and $\bar{X}$ and $\bar{Y}$ are the

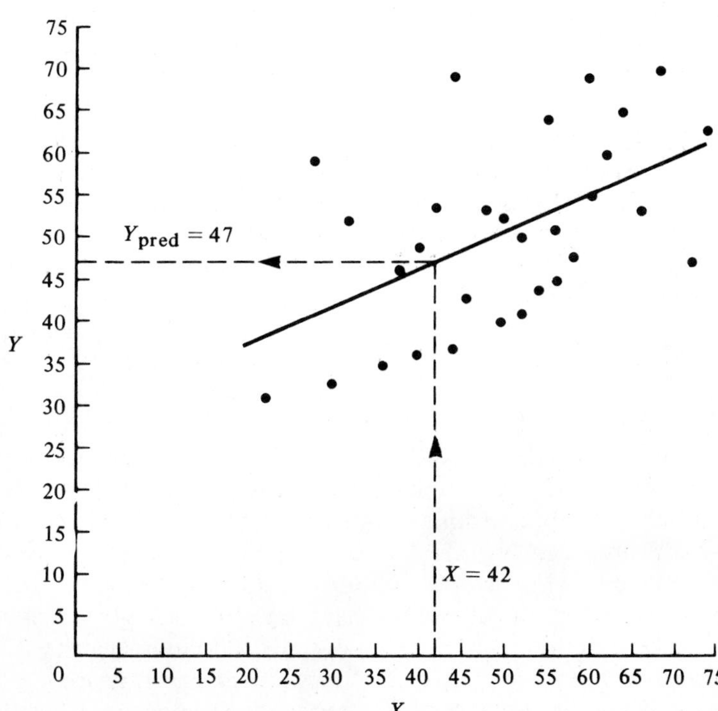

Graphical Plot of Data in Table 1–6, Showing Line of Regression of *Y* on *X*. **FIGURE 1–5**

means of X and Y, respectively. From the data in Table 1–6, the values of the five statistics are computed as $r = .52$, $s_x = 13.19$, $s_y = 11.04$, $\overline{X} = 49.93$, and $\overline{Y} = 50.37$. Entering these numbers into formula 1.7 and simplifying, $Y_{\text{pred}} = .44X + 28.64$. This is the equation of the straight line (the *regression line*) drawn through the score points in Figure 1–5. Using this equation, a person's score on variable Y can be predicted with better than chance accuracy from her or his score on variable X. For example, as illustrated graphically by the dashed lines in Figure 1–5, if $X = 42$, $Y_{\text{pred}} = .44(42) + 28.64 = 47.12$. Consequently, if a person's score on X is 42, the best prediction of his or her score on Y is approximately 47.

Factor Analysis

In addition to facilitating the process of prediction, the method of correlation is useful in the field of testing because the pattern of correlations among a group of tests may provide information on the nature of the psychological characteristics, or factors, being measured by more than one test. The statistical analysis of a group of correlations among tests into a set of common factors, the number of factors being smaller than the number of tests, is known as *factor analysis.* The results of factor analyses have led to a number of interesting theories concerning the structure of mental abilities and personality. But since factor analysis is a bit complicated, and the reader has probably had enough statistics for now, a discussion of this important topic will be postponed until Chapter 9.

Throughout the book, correlations between the scores of the same group of examinees on two different tests, the scores of two different groups of examinees on the same test, and the scores of the same group of examinees administered the same test on two different occasions will be considered. As will be seen in chapters 3 and 4, correlation coefficients are important both in designing tests and in determining their reliabilities and validities after they have been constructed.

SUMMARY

The roots of psychological testing and assessment can be traced to ancient China and Greece, although a concerted, scientific approach to the measurement of human differences in abilities and personality was not made until the late nineteenth century in England, France, Germany, and the United States. Testing has grown rapidly during the twentieth century, and psychological tests are now used extensively in education, business, the military, government, and in clinical situations. Of the many sources of information about tests, *The Mental Measurements Yearbook* is the most comprehensive. Tests are classified in various ways—standardized versus nonstandardized, individual versus group, speed versus power, objective versus nonobjective, verbal versus nonverbal, paper-and-pencil versus performance, and cognitive versus affective.

Statistical analysis of test scores begins with the construction of a frequency distribution showing the number of examinees who make each score or fall within a certain score range. A frequency distribution may be represented pictorially by a histogram or a frequency polygon. The normal curve is a theoretical, symmetric frequency polygon basic to much test theory and is used in determining certain types of norms. Asymmetric frequency distributions may be skewed to the right (positively skewed) or to the left (negatively skewed).

Three measures of the average score—the mode (most frequently occurring score), the median (score below which 50 percent of the scores fall), and the arithmetic mean (sum of the scores divided by the number of scores)—can be computed from raw scores or from a frequency distribution. Three measures of variability or spread are the range, the semi-interquartile range, and the standard deviation. The standard deviation is most often used and is the appropriate measure of variability when the arithmetic mean is the average. Raw scores can be converted to standard z scores, as well as percentiles, quartiles, and deciles.

The product-moment correlation coefficient, a number between -1.00 (perfect negative relationship) and $+1.00$ (perfect positive relationship), is a measure of the relationship between two variables. A significant correlation between two variables facilitates the prediction of a person's score on one variable from his or her score on the other variable, but it does not imply that either variable causes the other. The dimensions or structure underlying a matrix of correlations can be determined by the methods of factor analysis.

EXERCISES*

1. Identify the contribution(s) made by each of the following men to psychological and educational testing: Alfred Binet, James M. Cattell, Francis Galton, Hermann Rorschach, Charles Spearman, Lewis Terman, Edward L. Thorndike, Robert S. Woodworth. You will need to consult books on the history of psychological and educational testing, such as Linden and Linden (1968), DuBois (1970), or Edwards (1974), in order to obtain more complete information.
2. Discuss the various ways of classifying tests, evaluating each of them.
3. Examine copies of *The Ninth Mental Measurements Yearbook* (Mitchell, 1985) and *Tests in Print III* (Mitchell, 1983), which are available in most college and university libraries. Also obtain a copy of the *Standards for Educational and Psychological Testing* from your instructor. Describe the various kinds of information contained in these reference sources.
4. Some writers, particularly in the physical sciences, have questioned whether test scores and other forms of psychological and educational measurement really deserve to be called "measurement" at all. After reading a discussion of the logic of mental measurement (for example, Aiken, 1973, sec. III), defend the thesis that mental measurement is true measurement.

*Answers to the quantitative exercises for all chapters are given in Appendix C.

5. The following is a frequency distribution of the test scores obtained by a group of fifty students:

Test score interval	*Number of students*
96–100	6
91–95	8
86–90	15
81–85	10
76–80	7
71–75	4

Draw a histogram and a frequency polygon, and then compute the arithmetic mean, median, mode, standard deviation, 25th percentile, 75th percentile, and semi-interquartile range.

6. Given two groups (*X* and *Y*) of thirty scores each,

X	Y	X	Y	X	Y	X	Y	X	Y
32	46	28	23	37	28	36	21	42	27
35	26	32	20	27	13	31	14	39	46
20	8	45	24	37	22	35	18	34	16
41	42	29	13	23	34	43	47	33	30
25	28	46	40	30	31	34	27	29	26
38	25	40	37	36	39	39	32	24	7

compute the following statistics: the arithmetic means and standard deviations of *X* and *Y* (use raw-score formulas); the product-moment correlation between *X* and *Y*; and the regression equation for predicting *Y* from *X*. Plot the scores and draw the regression line of *Y* on *X*.

7. Referring to Appendix B, find the percentage of the area under the normal curve falling below each of the following *z* scores: −1.96, −1.64, .00, 1.64, 1.96. Next, find the *z* scores below which 10 percent, 20 percent, 30 percent, 40 percent, 60 percent, 70 percent, 80 percent, and 90 percent of the area under the normal curve falls.

8. Whenever the frequency distribution of a group of scores is markedly skewed in either a positive or a negative direction, the median is considered to be a more appropriate, or less biased, measure of the average score than the arithmetic mean. Why?

SUGGESTED READINGS

Buros, O. K. (1977). Fifty years in testing: Some reminiscences, criticism, and suggestions. *Educational Researcher, 6*(7), 9–15.

Cattell, J. M. (1890). Mental tests and measurements. *Mind, 15,* 373–380.

DuBois, P. H. (1970). *The history of psychological testing.* Boston: Allyn & Bacon.

Edwards, A. J. (1974). *Individual mental testing. Part I: History and theories.* Scranton, PA: Intext Educational Publishers.

Galton, F. (1879). Psychometric experiments. *Brain, 2,* 149–162.

Linden, K. W., & Linden, J. D. (1968). *Modern mental measurement: A historical perspective.* Boston: Houghton Mifflin.

McCall, R. B. (1986). *Fundamental statistics for behavioral sciences.* 4th ed. San Diego, CA: Harcourt Brace Jovanovich.

Miyazaki, I. (1976). *China's examination hell.* Trans C. Shirokauer. New York: Weatherhill.

Pagano, R. R. (1986). *Understanding statistics in the behavioral sciences.* 2d ed. St. Paul, MN: West.

Resnick, D. (1982). History of educational testing. In: A. K. Wigdor & W. R. Garner (Eds.), *Ability testing: Uses, consequences, and controversies. Part II: Documentation section* (pp. 173–194). Washington, DC: National Academy Press.

Chapter 2

Test Design and Construction

The amount of effort involved in constructing an educational or psychological test varies with the type of test and the purposes for which it is intended. Most classroom teachers probably spend relatively little time preparing essay or short-answer tests for evaluating pupil progress in a unit of instruction. On the other hand, the ability and personality assessment devices designed by specialists in psychological measurement usually require the efforts of many people working for extended periods of time.

The procedures employed in constructing a test also vary with the type of test and the aims of the users. The preparation of a paper-and-pencil inventory of interests or personality characteristics presents problems different from those encountered in constructing a test of achievement or aptitude. Similarly, the complex procedures followed by professional test designers are unfamiliar to the majority of teachers. But whatever the kind of test or the goals of the users may be, some content planning is necessary before the items comprising the test are written.

PLANNING A TEST

Constructing a test demands careful consideration of its specific purposes. Tests can serve many different functions, and the test-construction process varies somewhat with the particular purposes for which the test is intended. For example, different procedures are employed in constructing an aptitude test, an intelligence test, a personality inventory or rating scale, and an achievement test. Ideally, however, the construction of any test begins by defining the variable(s) or construct(s) to be measured and specifying the test content.

Screening Tests

When a test designer constructs an aptitude test to screen applicants for a particular job, he or she frequently must make a detailed analysis of the activities comprising the job before writing items designed to forecast job performance. Such a task analysis, or *job analysis,* consists of specifying the components of the job so that the test situations or items can be devised to predict employee performance. These specifications may include *critical incidents*—behaviors critical to successful or unsuccessful performance—as well as other information describing job activities. Since the description of a particular job typically is long and involved, the final test will not measure all aspects of employee performance. It will deal with only a sample of behaviors important to the job, but, it is hoped, a sample representative of the total process.

Intelligence Tests

Procedures for designing intelligence tests are described in detail in Chapter 7. As in constructing any other test, a pool of items that presumably measure some aspect of the construct "intelligence" is assembled. Selection of items for the final test is then made on the basis of the relationships of item responses to criteria such as chronological age and the interrelationships of the test items themselves.

Personality Inventories and Scales

A variety of approaches, some based on common (or educated) sense, others on personality theories, and still others on statistical procedures, have been employed in the construction of personality inventories and rating scales. As described in Chapters 12 and 13, many recently published personality inventories have been constructed by combining these approaches, using one or more of them at various stages of instrument development.

Achievement Tests

More attention has been devoted to procedures for constructing scholastic or academic achievement tests than to other types of tests, presumably because these kinds of tests are more widely administered than other psychological and educational assessment instruments. Despite the widespread usage of achievement tests, classroom teachers, who presumably are well acquainted with the subject matter they teach, typically devote insufficient time to the preparation of tests to evaluate student progress. Too often teachers view testing as a disagreeable adjunct to teaching rather than as an integral part of the instructional process. Used effectively, however, the results of tests serve not only to evaluate and motivate students but also to inform teachers and school administrators of the extent to which the objectives of instruction have been attained. By serving as a source of information on the effectiveness of the school curriculum and teaching procedures, test results can contribute to the modification and planning of instruction for individual students or entire classes.

Questions for Test Planners

The planner of a classroom achievement test should begin by answering the following questions:

1. What are the topics and materials on which the students are to be tested?
2. What kinds of questions should be constructed?
3. What item and test formats or layouts should be used?
4. When, where, and how should the test be given?
5. How should the completed test papers be scored and evaluated?

Questions 1–3 will be discussed in this chapter and questions 4–5 in Chapter 3.

Taxonomies of Educational Objectives

Just as the construction of a screening test for use in personnel selection requires a preliminary job analysis, the preparation of a test to measure specific instructional objectives is most effective when the behaviors to be assessed are clearly defined at the outset. In recent years, much attention has been given to formal, standard systems for classifying the cognitive and affective objectives of educational instruction. The categories of four such outlines of taxonomies of cognitive objectives are listed in Table 2–1. The six major categories of the first taxonomy, Bloom and Krathwohl's (1956) *Taxonomy of Educational Objectives: The Cognitive Domain,* are listed in order from least to most complex. These six categories are not exclusive but rather progressively inclusive. For example, both "Knowledge" (category I) and "Comprehension" (category II) are basic to "Application" (category III) and therefore are included in the third category. Descriptions of the categories in this taxonomy are given in Table 2–2.

The second taxonomy listed in Table 2–1, that proposed by Gerlach and Sullivan (1967), emphasizes the behavior of the examinee. In *identifying,* the examinee must indicate which member of a set belongs in a particular category.

TABLE 2–1 Illustrative Outlines of Cognitive Objectives

Bloom and Krathwohl (1956)	*Gerlach and Sullivan (1967)*
Knowledge	Identifying
Comprehension	Naming
Application	Describing
Analysis	Constructing
Synthesis	Ordering
Evaluation	Demonstrating

Educational Testing Service (1965)
- Remembering
- Understanding
- Thinking

Ebel (1979)
- Understanding of terminology (or vocabulary)
- Understanding of fact and principle (or generalization)
- Ability to explain or illustrate (understanding of relationships)
- Ability to calculate (numerical problems)
- Ability to predict (what is likely to happen under specified conditions)
- Ability to recommend appropriate action (or some specific practical problem situations)
- Ability to make an evaluative judgment

In *naming,* the correct verbal label for a referent or set of referents is supplied by the examinee. In *describing,* relevant categories of objects, events, properties, or relationships are reported by the examinee. In *constructing,* the examinee creates a product according to specifications. In *ordering,* the examinee arranges two or more referents in a specified order; in *demonstrating,* he or she performs behaviors to accomplish a specified task.

Following any of the outlines listed in Table 2–1 should encourage the test designer to go beyond simple recognitive or rote memory items and construct a number of test items to measure higher-order educational objectives that require some thought. The following items, which may be presented in either essay or objective test format, are illustrative:

> What is the formula for computing the standard error of measurement? *(Knowledge)*
>
> Examine the graph and determine how many items must be added to a fifty-item test to increase its reliability from .60 to .80. *(Comprehension)*
>
> Compute the standard error of estimate for a test having a correlation of .70 with a criterion having a standard deviation of 10. *(Application)*
>
> Differentiate between a classroom achievement test and a standardized achievement test in terms of what each measures and how each is used. *(Analysis)*

Categories of the *Taxonomy of Educational Objectives: Cognitive Domain* **TABLE 2–2**

I. *Knowledge* involves the recall of specific facts. Sample verbs in knowledge items are *define, identify, list,* and *name.* A knowledge item is: "List the six major categories of *The Taxonomy of Educational Objectives: The Cognitive Domain.*"
II. *Comprehension* means understanding the meaning or purpose of something. Sample verbs in comprehension items are *convert, explain,* and *summarize.* A comprehension item is: "Explain what the test reviewer means when he says that the test is unreliable."
III. *Application* involves the use of information and ideas in new situations. Sample verbs in application items are *compute, determine,* and *solve.* A sample application item is: "Compute the mean and standard deviation of the following group of scores."
IV. *Analysis* is breaking down something to reveal its structure and the interrelationships among its parts. Sample verbs are *analyze, differentiate,* and *relate.* A sample analysis item is: "Analyze this instructional unit into its several behavioral and content categories."
V. *Synthesis* is combining various elements or parts into a structural whole. Sample verbs are *design, devise, formulate,* and *plan.* A sample synthesis item is: "Design a table of specifications for a test on elementary statistics."
VI. *Evaluation* is making a judgment based on reasoning. Sample verbs are *compare, critique, evaluate,* and *judge.* A sample evaluation item is: "Evaluate the procedure used in standardizing this test."

Source: From *Taxonomy of Educational Objectives: the Classification of Educational Goals: Handbook I: The Cognitive Domain* by Benjamin S. Bloom et al. Copyright © 1964 by Longman Inc. Reprinted by permission of Longman Inc., New York.

Formulate a theory relating interests to personality, citing appropriate supporting research evidence. *(Synthesis)*
Evaluate the criticisms of Ralph Nader and Allen Nairn concerning the Scholastic Aptitude Test (SAT). *(Evaluation)*

Affective and Psychomotor Objectives

An important function of education is instilling certain attitudes, values, and other affective states in the learner. A completely satisfactory method of classifying the affective objectives of instruction does not exist, but proposals have been made. One such classification system is the *Taxonomy of Educational Objectives: Affective Domain* (Krathwohl, Bloom & Masia, 1964). The major categories of this taxonomy are: I. Receiving or Attending, II. Responding or Participating, III. Valuing or Believing in the Worth of Something, IV. Organizing Values into a System, V. Characterization by a Value or Value Complex.

Taxonomies of instructional objectives in the psychomotor domain have also been proposed (e.g., Simpson, 1966; Harrow, 1972). The six categories in

Harrow's Taxonomy of the Psychomotor Domain, for example, are Reflex Movements, Basic-Fundamental Movements, Perceptual Abilities, Physical Abilities, Skilled Movements, and Nondiscursive Communication.

Table of Specifications

Most test designers do not adhere rigidly to a formal taxonomy in specifying the objectives to be measured by a test. Nevertheless, it is helpful in planning a test to construct a two-way table of specifications. In constructing such a table, the behavioral objectives to be measured are listed as row headings and the content (topical) objectives as column headings. Then the descriptions of specific items falling under the appropriate row and column headings are written in the body (cells) of the table.

A table of specifications should be fairly detailed in terms of the knowledge and skills that examinees are expected to demonstrate, but it is important not to place undue emphasis on one particular objective. It may be easier to construct items that sample knowledge of terms and facts than items measuring the ability to analyze and evaluate, but items that measure attainments in the last two categories should also be included.

Table 2–3 is a table of specifications for a unit on the preparation, administration, and item analysis of tests. Notice that the percentage of the total number of test items to be devoted to each topic is given in parentheses below the particular topic. Once a set of objectives for a course of study has been decided on and a topic outline prepared, test items can be constructed to measure the extent to which students have attained the objectives listed for each topic.

Certain types of test items are more appropriate than others for measuring specific objectives. Short-answer and completion items, for example, lend themselves well to the measurement of knowledge of terminology, but they are inadequate in assessing higher-order cognitive skills and abilities. Consequently, the table of specifications for a test should be referred to in deciding what varieties of items, and how many of each, are appropriate. Practical considerations such as cost, time available for administration, item arrangement, and testing conditions must also be taken into account in planning a test.

PREPARING TEST ITEMS

The primary goal of test planning is preparation of a detailed outline, such as a table of specifications, to serve as a guide in constructing items to assess or predict certain objectives. Once a table of specifications or some other outline of the test has been prepared, the next step is to construct the items making up the body of the test. It is generally recommended that, on objective tests, about 20 percent more items than are actually needed be written initially so an adequate number of good items will be available for the final version of the test. Commercial testing organizations such as Educational Testing Service em-

TABLE 2–3 **Table of Specifications for a Test on the Preparation and Administration of Tests**

Behavioral objective	*Content (topic)*				
	Test preparation (16%)	*Test construction (26%)*	*Administration (14%)*	*Scoring (22%)*	*Item analysis (22%)*
Knowledge of terminology	Job analysis; critical incidents; representative sample (3 items)	Matching item; spiral omnibus; response set (5 items)	Rapport; halo effect (2 items)	Strip key; composite score; machine scoring (3 items)	Criterion; internal consistency; test homogeneity (3 items)
Knowledge of specific facts	Categories in "Taxonomy of Educational Objectives" (2 items)	Advantages and disadvantages of essay items and objective items (4 items)	Factors affecting test performance (3 items)	Rules for scoring essay and objective tests (3 items)	Methods of determining item validity; purposes of item analysis (3 items)
Comprehension	Explanation of the purposes of making a test plan (2 items)	(0 items)	(0 items)	Effects of weighting on total score (1 item)	Explanation of relationship between p and D (1 item)
Application	Specifications for a unit on testing (1 item)	Examples of multiple-choice items to measure comprehension, application, analysis, synthesis, and evaluation (4 items)	Directions for a test (2 items)	Correction for guessing; confidence weighting; use of nomograph for scoring rearrangement items (4 items)	Computation of difficulty and discrimination indexes; distribution of responses to distracters (4 items)
Total	(8 items)	(13 items)	(7 items)	(11 items)	(11 items)

ploy as item writers persons who possess both knowledge of the subject matter of the test and skill in writing items. Anyone desiring to learn how to construct good test items can profit from inspecting a sample of items in published standardized tests because they are among the best.

All test items represent methods of obtaining information about individuals, but the amount and kind of information varies with the nature of the tasks posed by different types of items. Telling examinees to compare the Battle of the Bulge with the Battle of Hastings demands a different kind of response from that obtained when they are simply told to indicate which of a series of listed events occurred in each battle. Complex integrating and organizing abilities are required by the first item, whereas only recognitive memory is needed to answer the second one.

Various methods of classifying items according to format, or the form of response required, have been suggested. *Supply* versus *selection, recall* versus *recognition,* and *constructed response* versus *identification* are ways of differentiating between items on which examinees are required to write or construct an answer and those on which they are to indicate which of several alternatives or options is correct. Another popular method of classifying items is *essay* versus *objective,* examples of which are given in Table 2–4. All essay items are of the supply type in that an examinee's answer is a constructed response. Objective items, however, may be of either the supply or selection type, depending on whether examinees must construct a response or merely select the answer from a list of alternatives. The crucial feature of objective items is not the form of the response but how objectively they can be scored. Two or more scorers of an essay item often disagree to some extent on the correctness of a given answer and how many points it should receive. But barring clerical errors, different scorers of an objective test will assign the same score to a given examinee.

Characteristics of Essay Items

The most important advantage of essay items is that they can measure the ability to organize, relate, and communicate—behaviors not so easily assessed by objective items. An essay test also takes less time to prepare, and it is unlikely that examinees will get items right by guessing. A shortcoming of essay tests is that the number of questions that can be answered in a typical class period (approximately six half-page answers in 50 minutes) may not provide an adequate sampling of examinees' subject-matter knowledge. Another drawback of essay items is their susceptibility to bluffing by verbally adept but uninformed examinees. In addition, the scoring of essay tests is rather subjective and time-consuming.

As a rule, essay items should not be used when it is possible to make the same evaluation with objective items. If essay questions are to be asked, the item writer should try to make the questions as objective as possible. This can be done by (1) defining the task and wording the items clearly (for example, asking the examinee to "contrast" and "explain" rather than "discuss"); (2) using

Examples of Various Types of Test Items **TABLE 2–4**

I. *Essay Items*
Directions: Write a half-page answer to each item.
1. Contrast the advantages and disadvantages of essay and objective test items.
2. Explain the reasons for performing an item analysis of a classroom test.

II. *Objective Items*
A. *Short-answer*
Directions: Write the appropriate word(s) in each blank.
1. The only thing that is objective about an objective test is the ______ ______________.
2. What is the first formal step in constructing a test to predict degree of success on a particular job? ______________

B. *True-false*
Directions: Circle T if the statement is true; circle F if it is false.
T F 1. The most comprehensive test classification system is that of *The Mental Measurements Yearbooks.*
T F 2. The social-desirability response set is the tendency to rate an examinee high on one trait simply because he/she is rated high on another trait.

C. *Matching*
Directions: Write the letter corresponding to the correct name in the appropriate marginal dash.

____ 1. group intelligence test	A. Binet
____ 2. individual intelligence test	B. Darwin
____ 3. interest inventory	C. Galton
____ 4. personality inventory	D. Otis
____ 5. product-moment correlation	E. Pearson
____ 6. sensorimotor tests	F. Rorschach
	G. Spearman
	H. Strong
	I. Woodworth

D. *Multiple-choice*
Directions: Write the letter of the correct option in the marginal dash opposite the item.
____ 1. Qualifying words such as *never, sometimes,* and *always,* which reveal the answer to an examinee who has no information on the subject of the item, are called
A. glittering generalities
B. interlocking adverbs
C. response sets
D. specific determiners
____ 2. Jimmy, who is 8 years, 4 months old, obtains a mental age score of 9 years, 5 months. What is his ratio IQ on the test?
A. 88
B. 90
C. 113
D. 120

a small number of items, all of which should be attempted by all examinees; (3) structuring the items in such a way that subject-matter experts will agree that one answer is better than another; and (4) having examinees answer each item on a separate sheet.

Short-Answer, True-False, and Matching Items

There are other types of objective items than the traditional four (short answer, true-false, matching, and multiple choice), but these four are the most popular. Among the advantages claimed for objective tests are that they can be easily and objectively scored, and, because less time is needed to answer an item, they permit a broader sampling of material than essay tests. In preparing objective tests, care should be taken to make the items clear, precise, grammatically correct, and written in language suitable to the reading level of the group for whom the test is intended. All information and qualifications needed to select a reasonable answer should be included; nonfunctional or stereotyped words and phrases should be omitted.

Although it is tempting to construct objective items by lifting statements verbatim from textbooks or other sources, this practice puts a premium on rote memory and should be avoided. Item writers should also be careful not to include irrelevant clues to the correct answers and to avoid interrelated or interlocking items. *Interrelated items* are those on which the wording of one item gives a clue to the answer to another item. When items are *interlocked,* it is necessary to know the correct answer to one item in order to get the other item right.

Short-Answer Items A short-answer item is a supply-type item on which examinees are required to complete or fill in the blank(s) of an incomplete statement with the correct word(s) or phrase or to give a brief answer to a question. In terms of the length of the constructed response, short-answer items fall somewhere between essay and recognition items. They are among the easiest items to construct, requiring that examinees supply the correct answer rather than simply recognize it. Short-answer items are especially useful in assessing knowledge of terminology, but they have serious limitations. They are not appropriate for measuring complex instructional objectives, and, because items sometimes have more than one correct answer, scoring is not always entirely objective. The following guidelines are useful in constructing short-answer items:

1. Use questions rather than incomplete statements.
2. If an incomplete statement is used, word it so that the blank comes at the end.
3. Avoid multiple blanks in the same item, especially if they make the meaning of the task unclear.

True-False Items One of the simplest types of items to construct, but probably the most maligned by professional testers, is the true-false statement. True-false items can be written and read quickly; therefore they permit a broad sampling of content. A notorious shortcoming is that they often deal with trivia or are constructed by lifting statements verbatim from textbooks, and consequently they encourage rote memorization on the part of examinees. Other criticisms of true-false items are that they are frequently ambiguous, cannot be used to measure more complex instructional objectives, and, by depending on rote memory, misdirect efforts to learn. Furthermore, because scores on a true-false test may be greatly affected by examinees' tendencies to guess and to agree (or disagree) when in doubt, the meaning of the scores may be questionable.[1] On the average, examinees will get 50 percent of the items on a true-false test correct simply by guessing. Scores are inflated even more when items contain *specific determiners*—words such as *all, always, never,* and *only* (which indicate that the statement is probably false) or *often, sometimes,* and *usually* (which indicate that the statement is probably true).

Ebel (1979) has argued that true-false items are not necessarily trivial or ambiguous and do not necessarily misdirect efforts to learn. In defending these items, he asserts that "the extent of students' command of a particular area of knowledge is indicated by their success in judging the truth or falsity of propositions related to it" (Ebel, 1970, p. 112). According to Ebel, such propositions are expressions of verbal knowledge, which he maintains is the essence of educational achievement. His claim can be questioned, but there is no questioning the fact that well-designed true-false items can measure more than rote memory. For example, by including two concepts, conditions, or events in a true-false item, the examiner can ask if it is true that they are moderately to strongly related (Diekhoff, 1984). Other possibilities are to ask if (1) one concept, condition, or event implies (is a consequence of) the other; (2) one concept, condition, or event is a subset, example, or category of the other; and (3) both concepts, conditions, or events are true. Such items can measure understanding as well as significant knowledge of concepts and events.

Whatever the objective may be, it is advisable to attend to the following suggestions in writing true-false items:

1. Make certain that the statements deal with important (nontrivial) matters.
2. Make the statements relatively short and unqualifiedly true or false.
3. Avoid negatively stated items, especially those containing double negatives.
4. Avoid ambiguous and tricky items.
5. As a rule, avoid specific determiners. If specific determiners are used to trip up unknowledgeable but testwise examinees, they should be included in true items as often as in false items.
6. On opinion statements, cite the source or authority of the opinion.
7. Make true and false statements about the same length, and make the number of true statements approximately equal to the number of false statements.[2]
8. Make wrong answers more attractive by wording the item in such a way that superficial logic, a popular misconception, or a specific determiner suggests that the wrong answer is correct. False statements having the ring of truth may also trip up unknowledgeable examinees (Ebel, 1979).

Matching Items In a sense, both true-false and multiple-choice items are varieties of matching items. On both types of items, a set of response options is to be matched to a set of stimulus options (premises). The distinction is that true-false and multiple-choice items have only one stimulus option (the *stem* of the item) and two or more response options, whereas matching items have multiple stimulus options and multiple response options. The examinee's task on a matching item is to indicate which response options go with which stimulus options. Matching is usually one-to-one (one response per stimulus), but it may well be one-to-many, many-to-one, or many-to-many. Examinees should be informed which of these applies.

Matching items are easy to construct and cover the material more efficiently than other types of items, but they usually measure only the rote memory of facts. In addition, the necessity of making the options homogeneous (all options are of the same kind, such as dates, places, or names) limits the type of material that can be fitted into a matching framework. Some guidelines for constructing matching items follow:

1. Place the stimulus (premise) and response options in a clear, logical column format, with the stimulus options in the left column and the response options in the right.
2. Number the stimulus options successively, and place letters (a, b, c, and so on) before the response options.
3. Use between six and fifteen options, including two or three more response options than stimulus options.
4. Specify the basis for matching clearly.
5. Keep the entire item on a single page.

Rearrangement Items These are types of matching items on which the examinee is required to sort a group of options into a fixed number of predetermined categories. The ranking item, in which options are to be arranged in rank order from first to last, is a special type of rearrangement item (see Table 3–2).

Multiple-Choice Items

The most versatile form of objective test item is the multiple-choice form: it can be used to measure simple and complex learning objectives at all grade levels and in all subject-matter areas. Scores on multiple-choice items are also less affected by guessing and other response sets than are scores on other types of objective items. Furthermore, useful diagnostic information may be obtained from an analysis of the incorrect options *(distracters)* selected by examinees.

Among the shortcomings of multiple-choice items are that (1) good ones are difficult to construct, especially items on which all options are equally attractive to examinees who do not know the correct answer; (2) they emphasize recognition rather than recall and organization of information; and (3) they require more time to answer and may sample the subject-matter domain less adequately than true-false items. It has also been alleged that multiple-choice tests favor shrewd, nimble-witted, rapid readers and penalize more thoughtful or profound examinees (Hoffman, 1962).

Guidelines for Writing Multiple-Choice Items The following guidelines should prove helpful in constructing the stems and options of high-quality multiple-choice items:

1. Either a question or an incomplete statement may be used as the stem, but the question format is preferred. Place blanks in incomplete statement stems at the end.
2. State the specific problem of the question or incomplete statement clearly in the stem and at a reading level appropriate for the examinees, but avoid taking questions or statements verbatim from textbooks.
3. Place as much of the item as possible in the stem. It is inefficient to repeat the same words in every option, and examinees have less difficulty with shorter options.
4. Employ opinion questions sparingly; when they are used, cite the authority or source of the opinion.
5. Four or five options are typical, but good items having only two or three options can also be written. With students in the lower grades, three options are preferable to four or five.
6. If the options have a natural order, such as dates or ages, it is advisable to arrange them accordingly; otherwise, arrange the options in random or alphabetical order (if alphabetizing does not give clues to the correct answer).
7. Make all options approximately equal in length, grammatically correct, and appropriate in relation to the stem. However, do not let the stem give away the correct option by verbal associations or other clues.
8. Make all options plausible to examinees who do not know the correct answer, but make only one option correct or "best." Popular misconceptions or statements that are only partially correct make good distracters.
9. Avoid, or at least minimize, the use of negative expressions (such as *not*) in either the stem or options.
10. Although a certain amount of novelty, and even humor, is appropriate and may serve to interest and motivate examinees, ambiguous or tricky stems and options should not be used.
11. Use "none of the above," "all of the above," or "more than one of the above" sparingly. Also avoid specific determiners such as "always" or "never."
12. Put the options in stacked (paragraph) rather than tandem (back-to-back) format, using numbers for items and letters for options.
13. Prepare the right number of items for the grade or age group to be tested, making each item independent (not interlocking or interrelated) of other items.
14. Make the difficulty levels of items such that the percentage of examinees getting the item right is approximately halfway between the chance (random guessing) percentage and 100 percent.

Simply following these guidelines, which are primarily the products of logic and experience rather than research, will not ensure the construction of a good multiple-choice test. The ability to write good test items depends as much or more on knowledge of the subject matter of the test, understanding what students should know and are unlikely to know about the subject matter, and the art or skill of asking questions rather than on following any set of rules. But even when the guidelines are not followed precisely, multiple-choice items tend to be fairly robust in their ability to measure knowledge and understanding.

Distracters According to Weitzman and McNamara (1946), the primary factor in determining how effective multiple-choice items are is the selection or construction of the incorrect options (distracters). Two methods, rational and empirical, have been used in selecting distracters. In the *rational* method, the test constructor makes personal judgments as to which distracters are appropriate. The *empirical* method entails selecting distracters according to the number of responses given to the stems of items when they are administered as open-ended statements. There is no consensus on which of the two methods produces better distracters, but examiner judgment appears to be at least as effective as the empirical method (Owens, Hanna & Coppedge, 1970; Hanna & Johnson, 1978).

Writing Complex Items Test constructors usually have more difficulty writing items to measure understanding and thinking processes than straightforward knowledge of the test material. There are various ways of constructing objective test items to measure the more complex objectives of instruction. Options such as "all of the above," "none of the above," "two of the above," and "all but one of the above" can make the examinee's choice more difficult. In addition, making all options correct (or incorrect) and requiring examinees to select the best or most nearly correct option for each item complicates the task. Other ways of making the task more demanding are (1) including multiple-answer items in which a variable number of options is correct and the examinee must indicate which (if any) are correct or incorrect, (2) having the examinee select an answer and improve upon it, and (3) having the examinee identify the correct set-up (such as an equation or other method of solution) on problem-solving tasks. Additional procedures for increasing the complexity of multiple-choice items are described in Table 2–5.

ASSEMBLING A TEST

After the test items have been written, it is always advisable to have them reviewed and edited by another knowledgeable person. Even the most painstaking efforts do not always produce a good test, and a friend or associate can frequently spot errors and make valuable suggestions for improving items.

Assuming that the test constructor has produced a sufficient number of satisfactory items, final decisions concerning several matters must be made before assembling the test:

Some Complex Multiple-Choice Item Forms TABLE 2–5

1. *Classification.* The examinee classifies a person, object, or condition into one of several categories designated in the stem:
Jean Piaget is best characterized as a __________ psychologist.
a. clinical
b. developmental
c. psychometric
d. social

2. *If-Then Conditions.* The examinee must decide the correct consequence of one or more conditions being present:
If the true variance of a test increases but the error variance remains constant, which of the following will occur?
a. reliability will increase
b. reliability will decrease
c. observed variance will decrease
d. neither reliability nor observed variance will change

3. *Multiple Conditions.* The examinee uses the two or more conditions or statements listed in the stem to draw a conclusion:
Given that Mary's raw score on a test is 60, the test mean is 59, and the standard deviation 2, what is Mary's *z* score?
a. −2.00
b. −.50
c. .50
d. 2.00

4. *Multiple True-False.* The examinee decides whether one, all, or none of the two or more conditions or statements listed in the stem is (are) correct:
Is it true that (1) Alfred Binet was the father of intelligence testing, and (2) his first intelligence test was published in 1916?
a. both 1 and 2
b. 1 but not 2
c. not 1 but 2
d. neither 1 nor 2

5. *Oddity.* The examinee indicates which option does not belong with the others:
Which of the following names does *not* belong with the others?
a. Alfred Adler
b. Sigmund Freud
c. Carl Jung
d. Carl Rogers

6. *Relations and Correlates.* The examinee determines the relationship between concepts 1 and 2 and indicates which of the concepts (a, b, c, d, etc.) listed in the options is related to concept 3 in the same way that concepts 1 and 2 are related:
Mean is to standard deviation as median is to
a. average deviation
b. inclusive range
c. semi-interquartile range
d. variance

1. Is the length of the test appropriate for the time limits?
2. How should the items be grouped or arranged on the pages of the test booklet?
3. Are answers to be marked in the test booklet, or is a special answer sheet to be used?
4. How will the test booklet and answer sheet be reproduced?
5. What information should be included in the test directions?

Test Length

The decision of how many items to include on a test depends on the time limits and the grade and reading level of the examinees. In tests at the secondary school level and beyond, a good rule is to allow 1 minute per item on multiple-choice or short-answer tests and 1 minute per two items on true-false tests. A 50-item multiple-choice or short-answer test and a 100-item true-false test are satisfactory for a typical 50-minute class period; approximately five or six half-page essay questions can be answered in this same amount of time. Using these time limits, 80 percent or more of the students in a typical secondary school or college-level class can be expected to finish the test. These recommendations concerning test length and administration time will need to be revised downward when testing elementary school pupils.

Arrangement of Items

It is sometimes heard that examinees show position preferences in selecting the correct answer to multiple-choice items. Examinees who do not know the correct answer may tend to select certain options (say *b* and *c*) more often than others (*a* and *d*). Although research (e.g., Wilbur, 1970, Jessell & Sullins, 1975) has failed to demonstrate a significant effect of such position preferences, it is a reasonable precaution to arrange multiple-choice and true-false items in the test booklet so that the answers follow no set pattern. On multiple-choice tests, putting the options in alphabetical order may accomplish this, but it is usually recommended that option order be randomized within items.

Placing short-answer items in groups of five or so reduces errors in taking and scoring the tests. On matching or rearrangement items, it is more convenient for examinees and for scoring purposes if all options appear on the same page. Finally, if answers to short-answer and essay items are to be written in the test booklet, sufficient space should be provided.

Concerning the layout of the test as a whole, it might be expected that the examinee's task would be facilitated if all items of the same type (multiple choice, true-false, and so on) and items dealing with the same topic were grouped together. However, although arranging items in groups according to type or topic may make test preparation, administration, and scoring easier, there is no evidence that it improves test scores.

It is also reasonable to suppose that test scores will be higher if subsets of items are arranged in order from easiest to most difficult. Being successful on easier items, which come first, presumably creates positive anticipations of success and hence encourages examinees to try harder on later, more difficult items. Again, however, research findings do not uniformly bear out this supposition. Although an occasional easy item may improve performance on subsequent items, in general arranging items in order of difficulty seems to have little or no effect on scores on multiple-choice tests (Allison, 1984; Gerow, 1980; Klimko, 1984). There are some exceptions to this conclusion, for example, speeded tests (Plake et al., 1982) and very difficult tests (Green, 1984; Savitz, 1985). In both cases, placing the most difficult items at the end of the test seems to improve scores somewhat.

A logical conclusion from research findings on the effects of item difficulty order appears to be that, in the case of easy or moderately difficult tests, the test designer should be less concerned with item arrangement and more concerned that the items are well written and measure what they are supposed to measure. When the test is very difficult or speeded, arranging items in easiest-to-most-difficult order may ensure more efficient use of time, as well as improve motivation, resulting in higher scores.

Answer Sheets

For most classroom tests, especially in the lower grades, it is advisable to have students mark their answers in the test booklets. This practice leads to fewer errors by examinees in finding the appropriate answer space. On objective items, having examinees write the appropriate letters or answers in marginal spaces to the left of the questions also facilitates scoring.

Separate answer sheets, which are easier to score, can be used at the upper elementary school level and beyond. Commercial answer sheets will have to be used if the test is to be machine scored (Figure 2–1). If answer sheets are to be scored by hand, the classroom teacher can easily make up an answer form and have it reproduced in quantity. To illustrate, an answer sheet for a fifty-item multiple-choice test might have a format like this:

```
 1. a b c d e        26. a b c d e
 2. a b c d e        27. a b c d e
 .................   .................
25. a b c d e        50. a b c d e
```

Examinees are instructed to check, blacken, or circle the letter corresponding to the correct answer to each item.

Reproducing a Test

Every educational institution has facilities for reproducing written or printed materials for classroom use. Mimeograph and Ditto machines are still found in some schools, but most schools and colleges have replaced them with photocopy machines. These machines can be used to duplicate test booklets in sufficient quantity for a specific test. If the same type of answer sheet is to be used for a number of tests, a large quantity can be reproduced in a single run of the machine and stored for later test administrations.

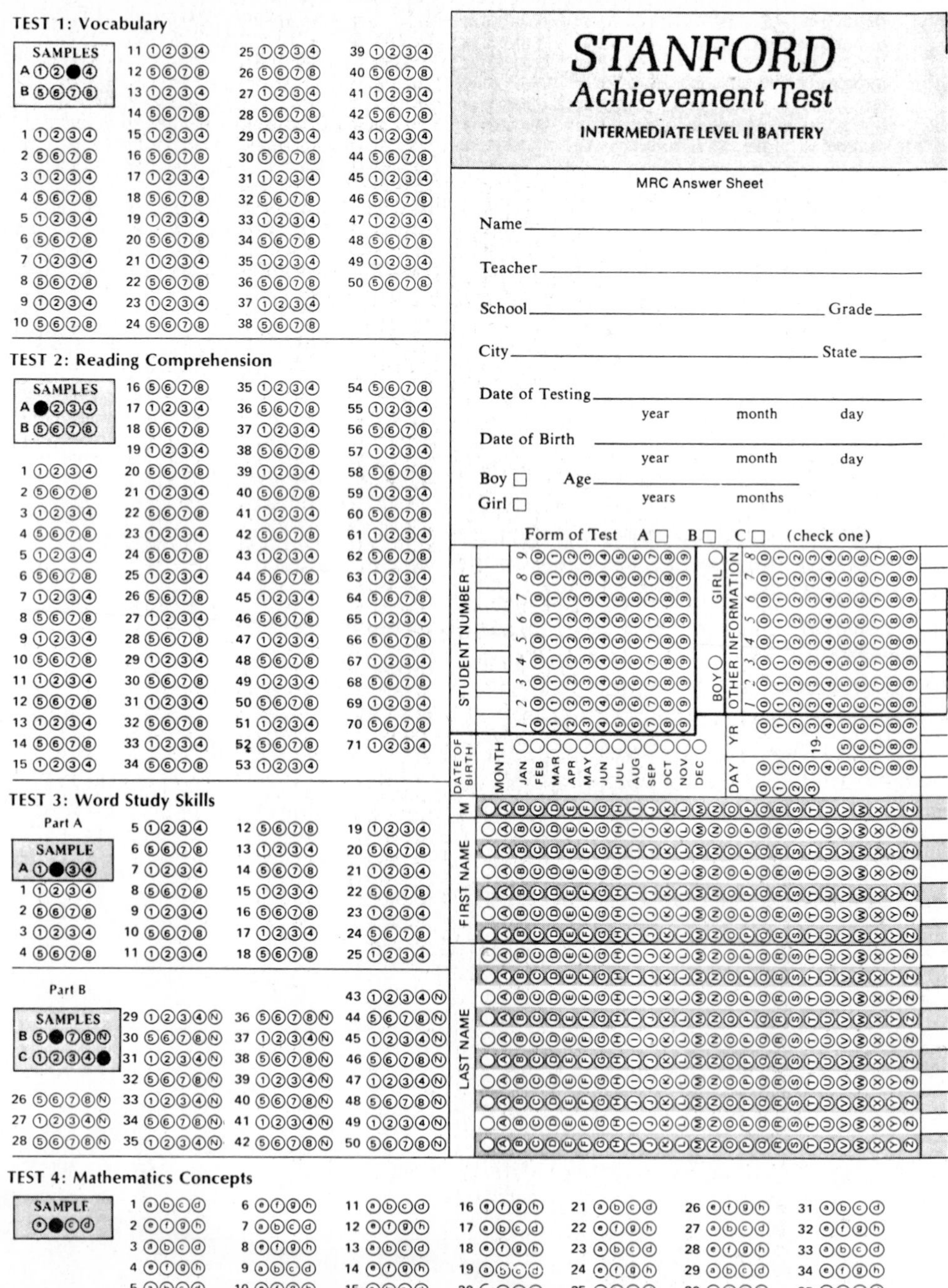

TEST 1: Vocabulary

SAMPLES
A ①②●④
B ⑤⑥⑦⑧

1 ①②③④ 2 ⑤⑥⑦⑧ 3 ①②③④ 4 ⑤⑥⑦⑧ 5 ①②③④ 6 ⑤⑥⑦⑧ 7 ①②③④ 8 ⑤⑥⑦⑧ 9 ①②③④ 10 ⑤⑥⑦⑧
11 ①②③④ 12 ⑤⑥⑦⑧ 13 ①②③④ 14 ⑤⑥⑦⑧ 15 ①②③④ 16 ⑤⑥⑦⑧ 17 ①②③④ 18 ⑤⑥⑦⑧ 19 ①②③④ 20 ⑤⑥⑦⑧
21 ①②③④ 22 ⑤⑥⑦⑧ 23 ①②③④ 24 ⑤⑥⑦⑧ 25 ①②③④ 26 ⑤⑥⑦⑧ 27 ①②③④ 28 ⑤⑥⑦⑧ 29 ①②③④ 30 ⑤⑥⑦⑧
31 ①②③④ 32 ⑤⑥⑦⑧ 33 ①②③④ 34 ⑤⑥⑦⑧ 35 ①②③④ 36 ⑤⑥⑦⑧ 37 ①②③④ 38 ⑤⑥⑦⑧ 39 ①②③④ 40 ⑤⑥⑦⑧
41 ①②③④ 42 ⑤⑥⑦⑧ 43 ①②③④ 44 ⑤⑥⑦⑧ 45 ①②③④ 46 ⑤⑥⑦⑧ 47 ①②③④ 48 ⑤⑥⑦⑧ 49 ①②③④ 50 ⑤⑥⑦⑧

TEST 2: Reading Comprehension

SAMPLES
A ●②③④
B ⑤⑥⑦⑧

1 ①②③④ 2 ⑤⑥⑦⑧ 3 ①②③④ 4 ⑤⑥⑦⑧ 5 ①②③④ 6 ⑤⑥⑦⑧ 7 ①②③④ 8 ⑤⑥⑦⑧ 9 ①②③④ 10 ⑤⑥⑦⑧
11 ①②③④ 12 ⑤⑥⑦⑧ 13 ①②③④ 14 ⑤⑥⑦⑧ 15 ①②③④ 16 ⑤⑥⑦⑧ 17 ①②③④ 18 ⑤⑥⑦⑧ 19 ①②③④ 20 ⑤⑥⑦⑧
21 ①②③④ 22 ⑤⑥⑦⑧ 23 ①②③④ 24 ⑤⑥⑦⑧ 25 ①②③④ 26 ⑤⑥⑦⑧ 27 ①②③④ 28 ⑤⑥⑦⑧ 29 ①②③④ 30 ⑤⑥⑦⑧
31 ①②③④ 32 ⑤⑥⑦⑧ 33 ①②③④ 34 ⑤⑥⑦⑧ 35 ①②③④ 36 ⑤⑥⑦⑧ 37 ①②③④ 38 ⑤⑥⑦⑧ 39 ①②③④ 40 ⑤⑥⑦⑧
41 ①②③④ 42 ⑤⑥⑦⑧ 43 ①②③④ 44 ⑤⑥⑦⑧ 45 ①②③④ 46 ⑤⑥⑦⑧ 47 ①②③④ 48 ⑤⑥⑦⑧ 49 ①②③④ 50 ⑤⑥⑦⑧
51 ①②③④ 52 ⑤⑥⑦⑧ 53 ①②③④ 54 ⑤⑥⑦⑧ 55 ①②③④ 56 ⑤⑥⑦⑧ 57 ①②③④ 58 ⑤⑥⑦⑧ 59 ①②③④ 60 ⑤⑥⑦⑧
61 ①②③④ 62 ⑤⑥⑦⑧ 63 ①②③④ 64 ⑤⑥⑦⑧ 65 ①②③④ 66 ⑤⑥⑦⑧ 67 ①②③④ 68 ⑤⑥⑦⑧ 69 ①②③④ 70 ⑤⑥⑦⑧ 71 ①②③④

TEST 3: Word Study Skills

Part A

SAMPLE
A ①●③④

1 ①②③④ 2 ⑤⑥⑦⑧ 3 ①②③④ 4 ⑤⑥⑦⑧ 5 ①②③④ 6 ⑤⑥⑦⑧ 7 ①②③④ 8 ⑤⑥⑦⑧ 9 ①②③④ 10 ⑤⑥⑦⑧
11 ①②③④ 12 ⑤⑥⑦⑧ 13 ①②③④ 14 ⑤⑥⑦⑧ 15 ①②③④ 16 ⑤⑥⑦⑧ 17 ①②③④ 18 ⑤⑥⑦⑧ 19 ①②③④ 20 ⑤⑥⑦⑧
21 ①②③④ 22 ⑤⑥⑦⑧ 23 ①②③④ 24 ⑤⑥⑦⑧ 25 ①②③④

Part B

SAMPLES
B ⑤●⑦⑧Ⓝ
C ①②③④●

26 ⑤⑥⑦⑧Ⓝ 27 ①②③④Ⓝ 28 ⑤⑥⑦⑧Ⓝ 29 ①②③④Ⓝ 30 ⑤⑥⑦⑧Ⓝ 31 ①②③④Ⓝ 32 ⑤⑥⑦⑧Ⓝ 33 ①②③④Ⓝ 34 ⑤⑥⑦⑧Ⓝ 35 ①②③④Ⓝ
36 ⑤⑥⑦⑧Ⓝ 37 ①②③④Ⓝ 38 ⑤⑥⑦⑧Ⓝ 39 ①②③④Ⓝ 40 ⑤⑥⑦⑧Ⓝ 41 ①②③④Ⓝ 42 ⑤⑥⑦⑧Ⓝ 43 ①②③④Ⓝ 44 ⑤⑥⑦⑧Ⓝ 45 ①②③④Ⓝ
46 ⑤⑥⑦⑧Ⓝ 47 ①②③④Ⓝ 48 ⑤⑥⑦⑧Ⓝ 49 ①②③④Ⓝ 50 ⑤⑥⑦⑧Ⓝ

TEST 4: Mathematics Concepts

SAMPLE
ⓔ●ⓒⓓ

1 ⓐⓑⓒⓓ 2 ⓔⓕⓖⓗ 3 ⓐⓑⓒⓓ 4 ⓔⓕⓖⓗ 5 ⓐⓑⓒⓓ 6 ⓔⓕⓖⓗ 7 ⓐⓑⓒⓓ 8 ⓔⓕⓖⓗ 9 ⓐⓑⓒⓓ 10 ⓔⓕⓖⓗ
11 ⓐⓑⓒⓓ 12 ⓔⓕⓖⓗ 13 ⓐⓑⓒⓓ 14 ⓔⓕⓖⓗ 15 ⓐⓑⓒⓓ 16 ⓔⓕⓖⓗ 17 ⓐⓑⓒⓓ 18 ⓔⓕⓖⓗ 19 ⓐⓑⓒⓓ 20 ⓔⓕⓖⓗ
21 ⓐⓑⓒⓓ 22 ⓔⓕⓖⓗ 23 ⓐⓑⓒⓓ 24 ⓔⓕⓖⓗ 25 ⓐⓑⓒⓓ 26 ⓔⓕⓖⓗ 27 ⓐⓑⓒⓓ 28 ⓔⓕⓖⓗ 29 ⓐⓑⓒⓓ 30 ⓔⓕⓖⓗ
31 ⓐⓑⓒⓓ 32 ⓔⓕⓖⓗ 33 ⓐⓑⓒⓓ 34 ⓔⓕⓖⓗ 35 ⓐⓑⓒⓓ

STANFORD
Achievement Test
INTERMEDIATE LEVEL II BATTERY

MRC Answer Sheet

Name ______
Teacher ______
School ______ Grade ______
City ______ State ______
Date of Testing ______ year month day
Date of Birth ______ year month day
Boy ☐ Girl ☐ Age ______ years months
Form of Test A ☐ B ☐ C ☐ (check one)

STUDENT NUMBER — GIRL ○ BOY ○ — OTHER INFORMATION

DATE OF BIRTH — MONTH: JAN FEB MAR APR MAY JUN JUL AUG SEP OCT NOV DEC — YR 19 — DAY

M — FIRST NAME — LAST NAME

FIGURE 2–1 Machine-Scorable Answer Sheet.
(Reproduced from MRC Answer Sheet for Stanford Achievement Test: 7th Edition. Copyright © 1982 by Harcourt Brace Jovanovich, Inc. Reproduced by special permission of the publisher.)

Test Directions

The directions for a test should tell examinees what they are supposed to do and how long they have. More specifically, the directions should indicate in relatively simple language the purpose of the test, the time limit, the method of recording answers, and the way in which the test will be scored. The directions should also indicate whether examinees should guess at answers when in doubt. A fairly detailed set of directions for a test on testing is as follows:

Write your name in the upper right-hand corner of the answer sheet; do not write anything in the test booklet. The purpose of this test is to determine your knowledge and understanding of test preparation, administration, and item analysis. There are fifty items, and you will be given 50 minutes in which to complete the test. Indicate your answer to each item by filling in the space on the answer sheet below the letter corresponding to the answer. Your score on the test will be the total number of items that you answer correctly. Therefore, you should make an informed guess when in doubt about the answer. Do not omit any items. If you finish before time is up, please sit quietly until everyone has completed the test.

ORAL TESTS

Oral testing is defined as an evaluation situation in which responses to questions are given orally by examinees; the questions are presented orally, in writing, or both. Oral achievement testing is more common in European educational institutions than in the United States, where oral testing has declined over time and is less frequent in the higher than in the lower grades (Graham, 1963; Hitchman, 1966).

It has been stated that students do not like oral tests and feel they are unfair measures of knowledge and understanding. On the other hand, teachers of speech, dramatics, English, and foreign languages often deplore the current inattention to the assessment of spoken language skills and feel that the consequence of this neglect is a multitude of graduates who cannot speak correctly, comprehensibly, or comfortably. However, while many teachers of languages and other subjects in which the development of oral language skills is important admit the desirability of oral exercises and evaluations, they also recognize that oral tests are inefficient and subjective (Platt, 1961; Crowl & McGinitie, 1974).

Since the early part of this century, oral achievement tests have tended to be perceived as inefficient and lacking in psychometric rigor. They have also been criticized as being too time-consuming, as providing a limited sample of responses, and as being poorly planned in most instances.

Advantages of Oral Tests

Despite the shortcomings of oral tests, even their critics admit that such tests possess some advantages over written tests. One advantage is the interactive social situation provided by oral examinations, permitting the evaluation of personal qualities such as appearance, style, and manner of speaking. The face-to-face situation also makes cheating, and perhaps bluffing, less likely (Ebel, 1979). Other advantages of oral tests are that they frequently require responses at a higher intellectual level than written tests and provide practice in oral communication and social interaction (Peterson, 1974). They also encourage more careful review of the test material and can be completed by examinees in less time than comparable written examinations. Oral examiners may be better able to follow the thought processes of examinees and determine the boundaries of their knowledge and understanding of the subject more readily. These boundaries can be determined by asking examinees to explain, defend, or elaborate on their answers. Finally, the time needed to prepare and evaluate oral answers may be less than for written tests (Glovrozov, 1974; Platt, 1961).

Oral tests are especially appropriate with primary school children and others who have reading or writing problems. Even at higher grade levels, administration of an occasional oral examination is justifiable when time and/or facilities for duplicating test materials are in short supply (Green, 1975). And in subjects such as speech, foreign languages, and dramatics, oral examinations are critical.

Oral versus Written Examinations

The fact that scores on oral achievement tests have only moderate correlations with scores on comparable written tests suggests that the two types of evaluation measure different aspects of achievement. In general, knowledge of specific facts can be assessed more quickly with objective written tests, so oral examinations should not contain large numbers of these kinds of questions. On the other hand, as with essay tests, oral testing is more appropriate when the questions call for extended responses (Green, 1975).

Because the achievements or behaviors assessed by oral tests are perhaps just as important as those measured by written tests, it can be argued that more attention should be paid to the main source of error in oral testing—the examiners or evaluators themselves. Oral examiners should have a thorough knowledge of the subject and be keenly aware of the kinds of oral responses desired. Furthermore, the categories used by the examiners in describing or rating examinees' responses should cite specific, observable behaviors rather than consisting of undefined, nebulous terms such as *creative potential, character, general ability,* or *interpersonal effectiveness*. Such vaguely defined variables are no more easily assessed by oral than by written tests (Ebel, 1979).

SUMMARY

This chapter has been concerned primarily with constructing, administering, and scoring achievement tests, but many of the principles that were discussed can also be applied to other kinds of psychological and educational assessment instruments.

The first step in constructing an achievement test is to prepare a list of behavioral objectives to be assessed. A table of specifications giving the number of items needed in each content (topical) category for each behavioral objective should then be constructed. Various taxonomies, or methods of classifying behavioral objectives in the cognitive, affective, and psychomotor domains, have been proposed. Bloom and Krathwohl's *Taxonomy of Educational Objectives: Cognitive Domain* has been the most popular of these.

Both essay and objective tests have advantages and disadvantages. Essay items are easier to construct, but objective items can be scored more quickly and accurately and provide a more representative sample of subject-matter content. Short-answer, true-false, multiple-choice, and matching are varieties of objective test items. Of these, multiple-choice items are the most versatile and popular.

In assembling a test, attention should be paid to such factors as test length and format, method of recording responses, facilities for reproducing the test, and directions for administration. The directions for administering a test include information on the purpose(s), time limits, scoring procedure, and advisability of guessing when in doubt. Oral tests are not employed as much as written tests, but when carefully planned, administered, and evaluated, they can provide information that is not usually obtained by other assessment methods.

EXERCISES

1. Choose a topic for a test in an area of interest to you, state your behavioral and content objectives, construct a table of specifications, and design a 1-hour objective test on the topic.
2. Design your own classification system for educational objectives in the cognitive domain. How does your system differ from those described in the text? What advantages and disadvantages does it possess over them?
3. Describe the relative advantages and disadvantages of essay and objective tests. For what purposes and under what conditions is each type of test most appropriate?
4. Why are multiple-choice items generally considered to be superior to other types of objective test items? Can you think of any situations in which true-false, completion, or matching items might be preferable to multiple-choice items?
5. Write five short-answer (completion), five true-false, and five multiple-choice questions on the following selection (Aiken, 1980, pp. 120–121):

Another reason for the shortage of psychometric data on the elderly is that older people, whose behavior is less susceptible to control by psychologists and educators, are frequently reluctant to be tested. There are many reasons for the uncooperativeness of elderly examinees, including lack of time, perception of the test tasks as trivial or meaningless, and the fear of doing badly and appearing foolish (Welford, 1958). Older adults, to an even greater extent than more test-conscious younger adults, do not relish performing tasks that make them appear stupid or that they perceive as having no significance in their lives.

Because of lower motivation to be tested in the first place, sensitivity and tact on the part of the psychological examiner are required to obtain valid responses in testing elderly people. Unfortunately, it is often questionable whether a technically proficient but young examiner can establish sufficient rapport with elderly examinees to communicate test directions adequately and stimulate them to do their best (Fletcher, 1972). Relatively few mental testers appear to have sufficient training and experience in the psychological examination of the elderly to do a credible job. Most examiners find, however, that once elderly examinees have agreed to be tested, they are as highly motivated to do their best as younger examinees (Welford, 1958).

Even when examinees are cooperative and motivated to do well, the time limits of many tests, the presence of sensory defects, and the distractibility and easy fatigability of many elderly people make it difficult for them to perform satisfactorily. For example, one of the most characteristic things about being older is that one's reflexes and physical movements tend to slow down. For this reason, explanations of the declining test scores of the elderly in such areas as learning and memory must take into account the fact that older people do not usually react as quickly as younger people. Although older people are usually at a disadvantage on timed tests, their performance improves significantly when they are given sufficient time in which to respond. Consequently, the elderly show little or no inferiority in comparison to younger people on untimed tests.

Sensory defects, especially in the visual and auditory modalities, can also interfere with performance in old age. Special test materials, such as large-face type, and trained examiners who are alert to the presence of sensory defects can be of help. Occasionally, however, an alleged sensory defect may actually be a mask for a problem in reading and auditory comprehension. For example, the writer had the experience of preparing to test an elderly man who, embarrassed by his poor reading ability, conveniently forgot his glasses and hence was unable to read the test materials.

6. What are the advantages and disadvantages of oral tests compared to written tests? Under what conditions are oral tests appropriate? How should they be designed, administered, and scored?

NOTES

1. *Acquiescence,* the tendency to agree when in doubt, is an example of a response set. *Response sets* are tendencies on the part of examinees to answer test items on the basis of their form—that is, the way in which the items are phrased—rather than on the basis of item content.
2. It can be argued that because false items tend to be more discriminating than true items, the number of false statements should be greater than the number of true statements. However, if the teacher follows this practice on successive tests, students may become aware of it and begin to answer "false" when in doubt about the answer.

SUGGESTED READINGS

Aiken, L. R. (1982). Writing multiple-choice items to measure higher-order educational objectives. *Educational and Psychological Measurement, 42,* 803–806.

Albrecht, J. E., & Carnes, D. (1982, November). Guidelines for developing, administering the essay test. *NASSP Bulletin, 66,* 47–53.

Cirn, J. T. (1986, Winter). True/false versus short answer questions. *College Teaching, 34,* 34–37.

Diekhoff, G. M. (1984, April). True-false tests that measure and promote structured understanding. *Teaching of Psychology, 11,* 99–101.

Ebel, R. L. (1975, Spring). Can teachers write good true-false test items? *Journal of Educational Measurement, 12,* 31–36.

Gerow, J. R. (1980). Performance on achievement tests as a function of the order of item difficulty. *Teaching of Psychology, 7,* 93–94.

Krathwohl, D. R., & Payne, D. A. (1971). Defining and assessing educational objectives. In R. L. Thorndike (ed.), *Educational measurement* (pp. 17–45). 2d ed. Washington, D.C.: American Council on Education.

Weiten, W. (1984). Violation of selected item construction principles in educational measurement. *Journal of Experimental Education, 52,* 174–178.

Chapter 3

Test Administration and Scoring

No matter how carefully a test is constructed, the results will be worthless unless it is administered and scored properly. The necessity of having established procedures or guidelines for administering and scoring psychological and educational tests is recognized by all professional organizations concerned with testing. A formal set of guidelines for test administration, scoring, and reporting is given in Chapter 15 of *Standards for Educational and Psychological Testing* (American Educational Research Association et al., 1985). These guidelines will not be listed here, but they are inherent in the discussion of administration and scoring in this chapter.

TEST ADMINISTRATION

The procedure to be followed in administering a test depends on the kind of test (individual or group, timed or untimed, cognitive or affective, and so on), as well as the characteristics of the examinees (chronological age, education, cultural background, physical and mental status). Whatever the type of test and the characteristics of examinees may be, factors such as the extent to which examinees are prepared for the test and their level of motivation, anxiety, fatigue, and health can also affect test performance.

Just as the preparedness, test wiseness, and motivation of examinees can affect their scores on an educational or psychological test, certain examiner and situational variables influence test performance. The skill, personality, and behavior of an examiner during the test can influence how well examinees perform. Formal licensing or certification by an appropriate state agency or supervision by a licensed examiner is required to administer most individual psychological tests. Such a requirement helps ensure that examiners possess the abilities needed to administer, score, and interpret psychological and educational tests.

Situational variables, including the time and place of testing and environmental conditions such as illumination, temperature, noise level, and ventilation, can also have an effect on test scores. For this reason, examiners must make careful preparations.

Examiner Duties before the Test

Scheduling the Test In scheduling a test, the examiner should take into account activities that examinees usually engage in at that time. Obviously, it is unwise to test during lunchtime, playtime, or when other pleasurable activities usually occur, are being anticipated, or even when enjoyable or exciting events have just taken place (such as immediately after a holiday). The testing period should seldom be longer than 1 hour when testing elementary school children or 1 1/2 hours when testing secondary school students. With preschool and primary school children, 30 minutes is often as long as examinees can maintain their attention. Consequently, longer tests may have to be administered to young children in more than one session.

In the case of a classroom test, examinees should be informed well in advance when and where the test will be administered, with what content it will deal, and what sort of test (objective, essay, oral) it will be. Students deserve an opportunity to prepare—intellectually, emotionally, and physically—for a test. For this reason, "pop quizzes" and other unannounced tests are usually not recommended.

Obtaining Informed Consent In many states, administration of intelligence tests and other psychodiagnostic instruments to school children requires the informed consent of a parent, guardian, or other legally responsible person. *Informed consent* is an agreement by an individual or his or her legal representative with an agency or another person to permit the collection of psychological test scores and other information on an individual and to use this information for a specified purpose. The requirement is usually satisfied by the signature of the responsible person on a standard form supplied by the school district or other relevant agency. The form specifies the purpose of the examination, the uses to be made of the findings, and the parents' or other guardians' rights and procedure for obtaining a report and interpretation of the results.

Becoming Familiar with the Test If the examiner also constructed the test, he or she will be familiar with the test material and the administration procedure. But because the administrator of a standardized test is rarely the same person who constructed it, the former will need to study the accompanying manual carefully before attempting to administer the test. Not only must the directions for administration be understood but the content of the test should be familiar to the examiner. To attain this familiarity, the examiner should take the test before attempting to give it to someone else. Finally, it is advisable to review the directions and other procedural matters just before administering the test. Test booklets, answer sheets, and other testing materials should also be checked beforehand and counted. "Secure" tests bearing serial numbers, such as the Scholastic Aptitude Test and the Graduate Record Examinations, should be inspected closely and arranged in order.

Ensuring Satisfactory Testing Conditions The test administrator should make certain that seating, lighting, ventilation, temperature, noise level, and other physical conditions are appropriate. A room familiar to the examinees and relatively free from distractions is preferred. A "Testing—Do Not Disturb" sign on the closed door may help to eliminate interruptions and other distractions. Individual testing should be conducted in a private room, with only the examiner and examinee (and, if necessary, the parent, guardian, or other responsible person) present. Special provisions may also have to be made for examinees who have physical handicaps or are physically different (for example, left-handed) from most others.

Minimizing Cheating Comfortable seating that minimizes cheating should be arranged. Although preferred, it is not always possible to place examinees one seat apart or in such a way that cheating is impossible. Preparing multiple forms (different items or different item arrangements) of the test and distributing different forms to adjacent examinees can assist in coping with cheating on group-administered tests. This procedure, however, does not eliminate the need for proctors. Several roving proctors should be employed whenever a large group of people is tested. Proctors assist in distributing and collecting test materials, as well as answering procedural questions, and their presence discourages cheating and unruliness during a test. The need for a certain number of proctors, and other procedures designed to guard against cheating, is taken quite seriously in the administration of secure standardized tests.

Examiner Duties during the Test

Following Test Directions On all standardized tests, the examiner is required to follow the direction for administration carefully, even when further explanation to examinees might clarify their task. Departures from the standard directions may present a different task to examinees than the test designers had in mind. Consequently, if the directions given to a group of examinees are different from those given to the group on whom the test was standardized (the *norm group*), the scores of the former will not have the same meaning as those of the latter. The result will be the loss of a useful frame of reference for interpreting the scores of the first group. The directions, which should be read slowly and clearly if given orally, should inform the examinees of the purpose of the test and how to indicate their answers but not what answers to give.

Establishing Rapport Although it is recommended that the examiner follow the printed directions closely in administering a standardized test, the examiner's behavior can have a significant effect on the motivation of examinees. Sometimes even a smile from the examiner provides enough encouragement to raise a person's score. On individual tests, where one has a better opportunity to observe an examinee than on group tests, the examiner is more likely to be able to detect low motivation, distractibility, and stress. An attempt may then be made to cope with these factors or at least take them into account in interpreting the scores. In group testing, where personal interaction with every examinee is not possible, the examiner is more limited in determining how well each examinee is doing and feeling. A good rule to follow on both individual and group tests is to be friendly but objective. Such behavior on the part of the examiner tends to create a condition of *rapport,* a relationship between examiner and examinees that encourages the latter to do their best.

Being Prepared for Special Problems There are circumstances in which an examiner needs to be especially active and encouraging. A testing situation creates a certain amount of tension in almost everyone, and occasionally an examinee may become quite anxious. Testing the very young, the mentally disturbed, the physically handicapped, and the culturally disadvantaged presents special problems of administration. In certain situations, questions and answers may have to be given orally rather than in writing or in a language other than English. Thus the examiner must be alert, flexible, warm, and objective, as well as familiar with the test material. Although these examiner qualities are not easily taught, experience in a variety of testing situations plays an important role in acquiring them.

Flexibility Some flexibility is usually permitted in administering nonstandardized tests and even certain standardized instruments. In testing with these measures, sensitivity and patience on the part of the examiner can provide a better opportunity for handicapped individuals and those with other special problems to demonstrate their capabilities. Other recommended procedures, which have been adapted from well-known instructional techniques, are the following:

1. Provide ample time for examinees to respond to the test material.
2. Allow sufficient practice on sample items.
3. Use relatively short testing periods.

4. Watch for fatigue and anxiety and take them into account.
5. Be aware of and make provisions for visual, auditory, and other sensory and perceptual-motor defects.
6. Employ a general amount of encouragement and positive reinforcement.
7. Do not try to force examinees to respond to test items when they repeatedly decline to do so.

Oral Testing Students frequently regard oral examinations with mixed feelings and often considerable apprehension. Consequently, efforts to calm fears and provide alternative testing methods for those who experience great difficulty coping with oral testing situations can assist in improving the effectiveness of these tests. Examiners who make special efforts to establish rapport with examinees discover that the latter may even come to enjoy oral tests.

Taking the Test

It is generally considered good educational practice to let students know in advance when they are going to be tested; telling them what kind of test will be given and what material it will cover is also recommended. As reasonable as these suggestions appear to be, announcing the type of test (essay or objective, for example) in advance does not invariably affect scores. It might seem as if examinees would do better if they were administered the same type of test they are told to expect, but this does not always happen (Kumar, Rabinsky & Pandey, 1979). It was found in one investigation, for example, that examinees did better when a recall test was expected, regardless of whether a recall or recognition test was actually administered (Balota & Neely, 1980). Other factors, such as mental ability, test wiseness, guessing, and careful reading and consideration of items, appear to have as much effect on test scores as knowing what type of test will be administered.

Test Wiseness In answering objective test items, examinees often use quite different methods from those intended by the item writer. Not all examinees read the items carefully, and they often fail to use all the information given (Williams & Jones, 1974). This may not be essential because students often recognize the correct answers to multiple-choice items without having read the material on which the questions are based (Preston, 1964). Apparently they are able to identify correct options by other means—by a process of elimination, by noting that an option is too broad or too narrow to be correct, or by seeing that it is worded incorrectly. Observations of students taking multiple-choice tests, and posttest interviews, indicate that although examinees sometimes answer an item simply by eliminating obviously incorrect choices, more commonly they make comparative judgments among the options. Knowledge of the teacher's idiosyncrasies is also an aspect of *test wiseness,* which appears to be a nongeneral, cue-specific ability (Evans, 1984) that develops as students mature and share information on test-taking skills (Slakter, Koehler & Hampton, 1970).

For example, the length, technicality, and "exoticness" of options act as cues to the correct answers (Chase, 1964; Strang, 1980; Tidwell, 1980). Boys appear to be more test wise than girls (Preston, 1964), and verbal items are more susceptible than numerical items to test wiseness (Rowley, 1974). Some aspects of test wiseness or test sophistication can also be taught (see Millman & Pauk, 1969; American College, 1978).

Changing Responses Examinees often must decide whether to change their initial responses to items. It is sometimes said that because one's initial answers tend to be right, going back over a test and changing answers that have already been deliberated upon is a waste of time and even self-defeating. The results of a number of investigations indicate, however, that test scores tend to be higher when examinees reconsider their answers and change some of them (Smith, White & Coop, 1979; Vidler & Hansen, 1980). Changing answers tends to raise scores more on difficult tests (Pascale, 1974) and with better students; males have also been found to do better than females when changing answers (Pascale, 1974). Answers are more likely to be changed from wrong to right than vice-versa (Vidler & Hansen, 1980), although the actual number of changed answers tends to be relatively small (Skinner, 1983). In any event, it is not a bad policy for examinees to review their answers when time permits.

Guessing Directions for objective tests often include a recommendation concerning whether to omit an item or guess when in doubt about the answer. Guessing, which is more likely to occur when items are difficult or wordy (Choppin, 1975), results in greater score inflation on true-false than on multiple-choice tests. Recommendations concerning guessing advise that examinees should guess only when they can eliminate one or more options or have some notion of the answer. Because examinees are almost always able to eliminate at least one option per item, leaving items blank rather than guessing usually results in lower test scores—whether or not scores are "corrected" for guessing.

Understandably, examinees guess less when they are informed that a penalty for guessing will be subtracted from their scores than when there are no directions concerning guessing or they are told to guess when in doubt. However, examinees do not always follow or even read test directions carefully, and those who read every word interpret and react differently to the directions. Regardless of what the test directions do or do not advise, some examinees are reluctant to guess when they are uncertain of the correct answer, a characteristic that might be labeled "intolerance of ambiguity" or "low risk taking."

Examiner Duties after the Test

After administering an individual test, the examiner should collect and secure all test materials. The examinee should be reassured concerning his or her performance, perhaps given a small reward, and returned to the proper place.

Some information on what will be done with the results and how they will be used can be given to the examinee and/or the responsible accompanying party.

Following the administration of a group test, the examiner should collect the necessary materials (test booklets, answer sheets, scratch paper, pencils, and so on). In the case of a standardized test, the test booklets and answer sheets must be counted and collated and all other collected materials checked to make certain that nothing is missing. Only then can the examinees be dismissed or prepared for the next activity and the answer sheets arranged for scoring.

TEST SCORING

Professional test designers do not wait until a test is constructed and administered before deciding what scoring procedure to use. Similarly, if a teacher-made test consists of a series of parts dealing with different content or different types of items, the teacher may wish to obtain separate scores on the various parts, as well as a composite score on the test as a whole. Differential numerical weights may be assigned to different responses. Decisions must also be made on such matters as whether to subtract a correction for guessing and whether to report the results in raw score form or to convert them in some way. For standardized tests, the classroom teacher does not have to make all these decisions; the answer sheets can be scored by machine. Even if they are to be hand scored, scoring stencils provided by the publisher can be used according to directions given in the manual.

Scoring Essay Tests

Essay questions can be made more effective by structuring the task clearly so that the interpretation of a question does not vary widely from examinee to examinee. Scoring can then be based on the quality of the answer. Similarly, an attempt should be made to structure and objectify the scoring of essay items so that a person's score depends less on noncontent, impressionistic factors and more on the understanding and ability demonstrated. Scoring on the basis of penmanship rather than quality of answers, being overly generous *(leniency error)*, and giving people high scores on an item simply because they make high scores on other items *(halo effect)* are among the errors affecting scores on essay tests.

A number of recommendations can be made for scoring essay questions so that the scores will be as objective and reliable as possible. To begin, the tester must decide whether to score the question as a whole or assign separate weights to different components. Whole *(global)* scoring is common, but it is perhaps more meaningful to use an analytic scoring procedure in which points are given for each item of information or skill included in an answer. In the first essay item of Table 2–4, for example, one point might be given for each correct advantage or disadvantage listed and a maximum of five points for the manner in which the answer was organized. The maximum number of points allocated to an item is determined not only by the examiner's judgment of the importance of the item but also by the assigned length of the answer. When the directions specify a half-page answer, the item should be weighted less than when a whole-page answer is required.

Whatever scoring weights may be assigned to specific questions and answers, it is advisable for the examiner to write out an ideal answer to the question beforehand. It is also recommended that the names of examinees be blocked out, if possible, before the test papers are inspected so they can be scored anonymously. Other recommendations are (1) score all examinees' answers to one question before going on to the next question, (2) score all answers to an item during the same time period; (3) if style (mechanics and quality of writing) and content are to be scored, evaluate them separately; (4) after a second person rescores the paper, make the final score the average of the number of points assigned by the two scorers; and (5) write comments next to answers and correct errors.

Corrections and comments written on classroom test papers are a valuable addition to the number of points or the grade assigned. A student is more likely to learn something from a test if the responses are corrected and commented on rather that simply assigned a number or letter grade.

Scoring Objective Tests

A unique advantage of objective tests is the efficiency and accuracy with which they can be scored. Whereas the scorer of an essay test has to spend hours reading the answers and weighing their correctness, a clerk can score an objective test quickly and accurately with a scoring stencil or machine. Therefore, the test papers are ready to be returned to the examinees soon after the test is administered—while the material is still fresh in their minds.

A strip key or stencil for hand scoring of test booklets or answer sheets can be prepared quite easily. A strip of cardboard containing the correct answers at positions corresponding to the spaces in the test booklet where answers are to be written makes a satisfactory strip key. A scoring stencil for use with a special answer sheet can be prepared from a blank sheet of paper or cardboard by punching out the spaces where the correct answers should be.

Machine Scoring Although the tests distributed by National Computer Systems and certain other commercial organizations can be scored only by machine, the majority of answer sheets for commercially distributed tests are scorable by hand or machine. After the test is administered, the answer sheets may be mailed to a special scoring service or returned to the distributor for machine scoring.

Objective tests have been scored by machines for over a half-century, and the increased availability of computers has made test scoring much more rapid, flexible, and economical. Optical scanners connected to computers can score hundreds of answer sheets in an hour. Numerous tests scoring services are now in business. Standard 15.5 of the *Standards for Educational and Psychological Testing* (American Educational Research Association et al., 1985) recommends that these services document the procedures they follow to ensure accurate scoring.

Human Scoring Errors Computer scoring of tests is not completely error free, and a section of standard 15.5 indicates that test scoring services should monitor their error frequency and report it on request. Standard 15.6 states that a corrected score report should be issued when errors are found in test scores. Compared with hand scoring, however, the error rates in computer scoring are small indeed.

Considering the fact that the scoring directions for many individual tests of intelligence and personality are not entirely clear-cut, it is not surprising that various scores may be assigned to the same test response. Although the variability of scores is probably greater with less experienced scorers, even experienced testers make mistakes. It has been found, for example, that errors in both administration and scoring occur when graduate students in psychology *and* professional psychologists administer individual intelligence tests (Franklin & Stillman, 1982; Ryan, Prefitera & Powers, 1983). In a number of cases, the errors are of sufficient magnitude to result in examinees' being misclassified as to their intelligence category. Other studies have found that examiners are affected in their scoring by whether they like the examinee or view him or her as being a warm person (Donahue & Sattler, 1971), and whether they perceive the examinee to be bright or dull (Sattler, Hillix & Neher, 1970; Sattler & Wingit, 1970).

Scoring Weights for Multiple-Choice and True-False Items It appears reasonable to suppose that on objective tests, as on essay items, the number of points assigned to an answer should vary with the kind of item and the quality of the response. There have been many studies of the effects of a priori weighting of responses to conventional objective test items, that is, assigning beforehand different numbers of points to different item types and responses. A number of researchers have found a priori weighting to be more discriminating and reliable than conventional scoring (Serlin & Kaiser, 1978; Willson, 1982; Hsu, Moss & Khampalikit, 1984). However, the advantages of a priori weighting do not seem to be justified by the increased scoring time and cost (Kansup & Hakstian, 1975). On tests of twenty or more items, simply assigning a score of 1 to each correct response and 0 to each incorrect response is as satisfactory as using differing scoring weights. Thus, the range of possible scores on a conventionally scored fifty-item multiple-choice or true-false test is 0 to 50.

It is possible, of course, that assigning different weights to different responses might be more effective if the type of response required of examinees were changed. For example, one interesting variation on the true-false format is to have examinees specify the degree of confidence they have in their answers (Ebel, 1965). Table 3–1 illustrates how this confidence weighting procedure works. Although the procedure may represent an improvement over conven-

TABLE 3–1 Ebel's Weighting Procedure for True-False Items

If the examinee indicates that	*And the statement is actually true, the score is*	*And the statement is actually false, the score is*
The statement is probably true	2 points	−2 points
The statement is possibly true	1 point	0 points
I have no idea	.5 point	.5 point
The statement is possibly false	0 points	1 point
The statement is probably false	−2 points	2 points

Source: Robert L. Ebel, *Measuring Educational Achievement,* © 1965, p. 131. Adapted by permission of Prentice-Hall, Inc. Englewood Cliffs, New Jersey.

tional 0–1 scoring of true-false items, the latter is probably satisfactory for most classroom tests.

Scoring Other Objective Items As with true-false and multiple-choice items, short-answer and matching items may be scored by assigning 1 point to each correct response and 0 points to each incorrect or omitted response. Because of the large number of different orders in which a group of items can be arranged, the scoring of rearrangement items presents a special problem. For example, the error of assigning to second place an item that actually belongs in first place is not as serious as placing the same item in fourth place.

Figure 3–1 is a simple computing chart *(nomograph)* that takes into account the fact that the seriousness of placing an item out of order depends on where it is placed relative to its correct position. To illustrate the use of the nomograph, assume that five cities are to be arranged in rank order according to population by assigning a rank of 1 to the largest city, 2 to the next largest city, and so on. The names of the five cities are given in the first column of Table 3–2, their correct ranks in the second column, and the ranks assigned by a hypothetical examinee (A) in the third column. The fourth column contains the absolute values of the differences between the correct rank for each city and the rank assigned by the examinee; the sum of the absolute values of the differences is 10.

To determine the score of examinee A on this item, referring Figure 3–1, the scorer marks a point at the appropriate value, 10, on the vertical *Diff* scale and a point on the curved *Number* scale at the value of the number of things ranked, 5. A straight line extended from the point at 10 on the *Diff* scale through 5 on the *Number* scale intersects the *Score* scale at a value of approximately 1. Therefore, examinee A's score on this ranking item is 1 (rounded off). The nomograph of Figure 3–1 may be used to score rearrangement items in which the number of things to be arranged is between two and twenty. The minimum score is 0, and the maximum score is equal to the number of things to be rearranged.

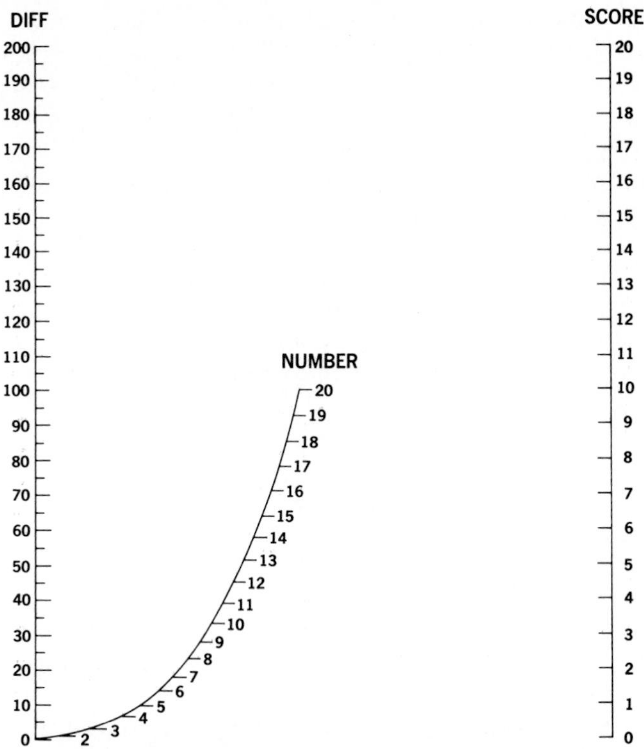

FIGURE 3–1 **Nomograph for Scoring Rearrangement Test Items.** (After Aiken, 1970, p. 90.)

Correction for Guessing After the total raw score on an objective test has been determined, a question arises as to whether the score represents an examinee's true standing or whether it has been inflated by successful guessing. Examinees do guess on objective tests, and their chances of improving their scores in this way, especially on items having few options, can be quite high. If an examinee does not know the correct answer and all options are equally attractive, then the chances that the correct option will be selected by guessing

TABLE 3–2 **Rank Ordering of Sample Rearrangement Item**

City	*Correct rank*	*Examinee A's rank*	*Absolute value of difference*
Boston	4	1	3
Chicago	2	3	1
Los Angeles	3	2	1
New Orleans	5	4	1
New York	1	5	4
			Diff = 10

are $100/k$ out of 100, where k is the number of options per item. Thus, the chances of blindly guessing the correct answer to a true-false item are 50 out of 100 (since $k = 2$ for true-false items). On a four-option multiple-choice item, however, the chances are only 25 out of 100 of guessing the correct answer. Obviously, guessing the answer to a large number of items will have a more serious effect on scores on true-false items than on multiple-choice items.

As an attempt to correct for the effects of guessing, on certain standardized tests a portion of the number of wrong answers is subtracted from the number of right answers. The reasoning behind correction-for-guessing formulas need not concern us here, except for the questionable assumption that examinees will guess blindly when in doubt. The most popular scoring formula when correcting for guessing is considered appropriate is:

$$S = R - \frac{W}{k - 1}, \tag{3.1}$$

where S is the corrected score, R the number of items that the examinee gets right, and W the number of items wrong. This formula has been criticized for yielding scores that are too low when examinees are less familiar with the test material but too high when they are more familiar with the material (Little, 1962, 1966). An alternative formula proposed by Little (1962) is $S = R - W/[2(k - 1)]$.

Professional testers generally agree that so-called correction-for-guessing formulas do not really correct for guessing and that they typically have little effect on the rank order of scores. Exceptions are when the number of unanswered items varies greatly from examinee to examinee and when certain items are more likely to be guessed at than others. The use of these formulas, which is similar to assigning different weights to different items, is not generally recommended in scoring classroom tests. The formulas are probably most helpful in scoring true-false and speeded tests, where guessing is more of a factor than on other types of tests. Negative scores, which occasionally occur when formula 3.1 is used with true-false tests ($S = R - W$), are usually changed to zeroes. Whether a correction for guessing is employed, the test directions should provide information on how the test will be scored.

Converted Scores Although it may not be worthwhile to alter raw scores on objective tests by differential weighting or correction formulas, the scores are often changed in other ways to make them more meaningful. As will be seen in the discussion of norms in Chapter 4, the interpretation of test scores is facilitated by transforming them to percentile ranks, standard scores, or converted scores.

Scoring Oral Tests Although there are greater possibilities of error in scoring responses to oral test questions than to objective test items, special forms for rating performance can improve the objectivity of scoring oral tests. Careful attention to the design of questions, construction of model answers to questions before administering the test, the use of multiple raters or scorers, and training examiners to avoid favoritism and other rater biases also can decrease errors in scoring oral test responses. If the time allotted to scoring is not critical, the accuracy with which oral tests are scored can be improved by tape-recording examinees' responses for later playback and (re)evaluation (see Aiken, 1983a).

Grading and Interpretation

After a test has been administered and scored, the scores must be evaluated. In the case of teacher-made tests, score evaluation usually implies the assignment of letter grades or marks. Grade assignment is a somewhat subjective, relative process, depending not only on the test scores themselves but also on the expectations of the teacher and the scores obtained by other students and classes. Some teachers grade strictly on the curve, others grade in terms of a fixed performance standard or criterion, but the majority probably employ a combination of curve and fixed-standard grading. In one curve-grading procedure, the *Cajori method,* A's are assigned to 7 percent of the examinees, B's to 24 percent, C's to 38 percent, D's to 24 percent, and F's to 7 percent. This method of grading, however, fails to take into consideration the facts that tests vary in level of difficulty and that the overall ability level of students varies from class to class. An alternative curve-grading procedure has been developed to set letter grade boundaries on classroom tests when the ability level of the class, the class's test performance relative to that of other classes, and the test scores themselves are to be taken into account in assigning grades. Interested readers should consult Aiken (1983b) for details of this method.

The traditional grading system, in which A is considered excellent or superior, B is above average or good, C is average or fair, D is below average or poor, and F is failing, is a form of score interpretation or performance evaluation. Every production and service organization, whether in the public or private sector, has standards that its students or employees are expected to meet. The standards may be flexible and forgiving, but at some time the student or employee must be evaluated positively or be penalized. The penalty for receiving a poor evaluation may take the form of remedial work, demotion, suspension, or even expulsion. The rewards for receiving a good evaluation include prizes, privileges, and promotions.

Letter grading implies the evaluation of scholastic performance by administering various kinds of achievement tests to students. Scores on other tests of ability and personality also require interpretation if they are to be used for certain purposes: for placement in special classes or jobs, for psychodiagnosis, and for psychological treatments and other interventions. Procedures for interpreting scores on such tests can be quite complex depending on the type of test and the purpose(s) for which it is administered. These procedures are described throughout this book, beginning with the discussion of norms in the next chapter.

SUMMARY

Procedures for administering and scoring tests vary to some extent with the type of test and the nature of the examinees. Of particular importance are that examinees be prepared for the test, motivated to do well, and relatively free from stress and other disruptive conditions. The examiner should be trained, familiar with the test, and have everything in order before attempting to administer it. In general, the testing situation should be physically and psychologically comfortable so the examinees will be inclined to do their best.

As a rule, examinees should be informed of the purpose of a test, where and when the test will be administered, as well as its format and the material with which it will deal. Examiners should follow the test directions carefully, taking precautions to minimize cheating, and prepared to handle emergencies and other special problems. Some flexibility is usually permitted in administering both teacher-made and standardized tests, but sharp deviations from the directions for administration will invalidate the use of norms on the latter type of test. Examiners should also attempt to establish rapport with the examinees, especially on individually administered tests.

Test wiseness, successful guessing, changing answers, and cheating are some of the factors that can inflate scores on objective tests; bluffing, a sophisticated writing style, and good penmanship can do the same on essay tests. The effects of test wiseness can be minimized by constructing test items carefully, avoiding cues such as item length, specific determiners, grammatical errors, stylistic giveaways, and nonhomogeneous (nonparallel) options. Correction-for-guessing formulas are sometimes used to reduce the effects of guessing, especially on true-false tests. With the possible exception of true-false tests, however, the conventional correction-for-guessing formula is usually not worth the time or effort to apply in scoring classroom tests.

Essay tests may be scored holistically or analytically, but in either case examinees should know how they are to be scored. Independent scoring of essay items and examinees is recommended, as well as separate scoring for content and style. In addition to a numerical score, written comments, corrections, and explanations are often helpful in providing feedback on essay test performance.

Many objective tests are scored by computers or other special machines. Machine scoring is generally superior to hand scoring in terms of speed and accuracy but less flexible. The scoring of many individual tests of intelligence and personality is less than perfectly objective and may result in serious errors on the part of professional testers and trainees alike.

The effect of assigning different scoring weights for different kinds of objective items and different responses to an item is a topic that has been widely researched. In general, a priori scoring weights are not recommended on tests consisting of twenty items or more.

Raw test scores are often converted to percentile ranks or standard scores for purposes of averaging scores, making comparisons among scores, and interpreting scores. Scores on classroom tests are also converted to grades, either by using a fixed set of percentages such as those specified by the Cajori method or in a more subjective fashion.

EXERCISES

1. What are the advantages and disadvantages of administering and scoring an essay test compared with an objective test? Of administering and scoring an oral examination compared with a written examination?
2. Define *test wiseness,* and describe test-taking behaviors that are indicative of test wiseness. What can a test constructor do to minimize the effects of test wiseness on test scores?
3. Question a group of your fellow students about the techniques they use in selecting the correct answers to items on a multiple-choice test when they do not know the test material very well. What techniques are most popular, and how effective are they according to the respondents?
4. You have undoubtedly observed that the speed of completing a classroom test varies substantially from student to student. Some students finish a 2-hour examination in less than 1 hour, while others continue working even after time is called. From your observations and discussions, what do you consider the major factors in determining how quickly students complete a test?
5. John takes a fifty-item, four-option multiple-choice test. He gets thirty items right and sixteen items wrong, and he leaves four items blank. What is his total score on the test, both corrected and uncorrected for guessing? If all items were of the true-false variety and he gave the same number of correct and incorrect answers as indicated above, what would his total score be—both corrected and uncorrected for guessing?
6. A test on British history contains an item consisting of a list of seven battles. Students are asked to arrange the seven battles according to their dates of occurrence, from first to last. The correct order is: Battle of Hastings, Battle of Bunker Hill, Battle of Yorktown, Battle of Trafalgar, Battle of Waterloo, Battle of the Marne, Battle of Britain. John lists the seven battles in the order: Waterloo, Hastings, Yorktown, Trafalgar, Marne, Britain, Bunker Hill. What is his score on the item? Jenny lists the seven battles in the order: Hastings, Waterloo, Yorktown, Bunker Hill, Trafalgar, Marne, Britain. What is her score? (Use Figure 3–1.)
7. Applying the percentages designated by the Cajori method, assign letter grades to the scores in the X and Y distributions in exercise 6 of Chapter 1.

SUGGESTED READINGS

Aiken, L. R. (1980). Problems in testing the elderly. *Educational Gerontology, 5,* 119–124.

Aiken, L. R. (1987). *Assessment of intellectual functioning* (pp. 57–70). Newton, MA: Allyn & Bacon.

Airasian, P. W., & Terrasi, S. (1985). Test administration. In T. Husen & T.N. Postlethwaite (eds.), *International encyclopedia of education* (vol. 9, pp. 5195–5198). New York: Wiley.

American College (1978). *Test wiseness: Test taking skills for adults.* New York: McGraw-Hill.

American Educational Research Association, American Psychological Association & National Council on Measurement in Education. (1985). *Standards for educational and psychological testing* (pp. 83–84). Washington, D.C.: American Psychological Association.

Hughes, D. C. & Keeling, B. (1984). The use of model essays to reduce context effects in essay scoring. *Journal of Educational Measurement, 21,* 277–281.

Lord, F. M. (1975). Formula scoring and number right scoring. *Journal of Educational Measurement, 12,* 7–12.

Naylor, F. D. (1985). Test-taking anxiety. In T. Husen & T. N. Postlethwaite (eds.), *International encyclopedia of education* (vol. 9, pp. 5209–5211). New York: Wiley.

Starch, D., & Elliott, E. C. (1912). Reliability of grading high school work in English. *School Review, 20,* 442–457.

Wang, M. W., & Stanley, J. C. (1970). Differential weighting: A review of methods and empirical studies. *Review of Educational Research, 40,* 663–705.

Chapter 4

Item Analysis and Test Standardization

After a test has been administered and scored, the examiner cannot always be certain that the test has done its job well. When a test is tried out initially, it is likely that a number of problems will be encountered. Whatever the type of test—standardized or teacher made, ability or personality—a "postmortem" or post hoc analysis of results is just as necessary as it is in medicine or any other human enterprise. Among the questions that need answering are: Were the time limits adequate? Did the examinees understand the directions? Were the environmental conditions appropriate? Were emergencies handled properly? Rarely is every problem or contingency that arises during a test anticipated. A post hoc analysis can provide information and motivation for meeting similar situations on future administrations of the test.

An important part of a post hoc analysis of a test administration is examining the responses to each of the items comprising the test. Some of the items may not have functioned effectively and will have to be discarded or revised before the test is readministered.

ITEM ANALYSIS

An analysis of the responses given by a group of examinees to the individual items on a test serves several functions. The major aim of such an *item analysis* is to help improve the test by revising or discarding ineffective items. Another important function served by an item analysis, especially with classroom achievement tests, is to provide diagnostic information on what examinees do and do not know.

Criterion-Referenced Tests and Mastery

The procedure employed in evaluating the effectiveness of test items depends to some extent on the purposes of the test. For example, the tester may be simply interested in determining how much an examinee knows of the test material, not in comparing the latter's performance with that of other examinees. In this case a student's performance is compared with a criterion or standard established by the classroom teacher or by institutional policy. The purpose of such *criterion-referenced testing* is not to discover where people score in relation to the scores of other people but rather to determine where each person stands with respect to certain educational objectives. A particular type of criterion-referenced test designed to measure attainment of a limited range of cognitive skills is known as a *mastery test.* A person's score on a mastery test, or any other criterion-referenced test, is expressed as a percentage of the total number of items answered correctly; a perfect score is 100 percent mastery of the test material.

Individual Differences and Item Validity

Since it is frequently difficult to obtain agreement on how much an individual should know about a particular subject or what constitutes mastery of the subject, a score on a psychological or educational test is more often interpreted by comparing it with the scores of other people. The history of testing is intertwined with the study of individual differences, and psychological tests have been devised primarily to assess the differences among individuals in cognitive and affective characteristics. People differ in their abilities and personalities, and it is these differences that psychologists attempt to measure with tests. The more accurately this can be done, the more precisely will an individual's behavior be predictable from test scores. Consequently, professional test constructors try to devise items that differentiate among individuals in whatever is being measured. By so doing, the variability among individuals in total test scores is increased, and a given score more accurately reflects an examinee's standing in relation to other people.

In assessing the usefulness of an item as a measure of individual differences in ability or personality characteristics, the tester needs some external criterion measure of the characteristic. If the test is being constructed to predict performance on a job or in school, then a suitable external criterion is an index of job performance (for example, supervisors' ratings) or school achievement (for example, teacher-assigned marks). The *validity* of an item for predicting the particular external criterion measure may be determined by computing the correlation between scores on the item (0s and 1s) and scores on the criterion measure. Many different types of correlation coefficients have been used for this purpose, the most common being the *point-biserial coefficient.* A formula for computing the point-biserial coefficient is

$$r_{pb} = \frac{(\bar{Y}_1 - \bar{Y})}{s}\sqrt{\frac{n_1 n}{(n - n_1)(n - 1)}}, \tag{4.1}$$

where n = the total number of examinees, n_1 = the number of examinees who pass the item, $\bar{Y}_1$ = the mean criterion score of examinees who pass the item, $\bar{Y}$ = the mean of all criterion scores, and s = the standard deviation of all criterion scores. The criterion may, of course, be total scores on the test itself.

To illustrate the computation of the point-biserial coefficient, assume that the total test scores of a group of thirty examinees have a mean of 75 and a standard deviation of 10. Also assume that the mean test score of the seventeen examinees who get item 1 correct is 80. Then applying formula 4.1, we have

$$r_{pb} = \frac{(80 - 75)}{10}\sqrt{\frac{17(30)}{13(29)}} = .58.$$

The higher the validity index (item-criterion correlation) of an item is, the more useful it is for predicting the criterion. Whether an item will be retained or discarded depends on how high the validity index is. Although items with validity indexes as low as .20 may contribute to the prediction of the criterion, items with higher indexes are preferred. Certainly an item with a validity index close to .00 or with a negative validity index should be revised or discarded. The usefulness of an item in predicting a criterion, however, depends not only on its validity index but also on its correlation with other items on the test. Items that have high validity indexes but low correlations with other items are best because they make a more independent contribution to the prediction of the criterion.

Item Difficulty and Discrimination Indexes

On classroom achievement tests there is usually no external criterion against which to validate items, so a different, *internal consistency,* procedure is employed. Although the item analysis of a classroom test, like that of any other test, involves determining the percentage of examinees who pass the item and the correlation of the item with a criterion, in this case the criterion consists of total scores on the test itself. A short-cut procedure is to divide the examinees into three groups according to their scores on the test as a whole: an upper group consisting of the 27 percent who make the highest scores, a lower group of the 27 percent who make the lowest scores, and a middle group of the remaining 46 percent. Using the scores of the upper and lower groups, the following statistical indexes are computed:

$$p = \frac{U_p + L_p}{U + L} \tag{4.2}$$

and

$$D = \frac{U_p - L_p}{U}. \tag{4.3}$$

U_p and L_p designate the numbers of examinees in the upper and lower groups, respectively, who pass the item, whereas U and L are the total numbers in the upper and lower groups.[1] The value of p is referred to as an *item difficulty index* and the value of D as an *item discrimination index*. To illustrate the computation of these indexes, assume that fifty people take a test. Then the upper and lower groups can be formed from the top fourteen and bottom fourteen examinees on total test score. If twelve of the examinees in the upper group and seven of those in the lower group pass item A, then $p = (12 + 7)/28 = .68$ and $D = (12 - 7)/14 = .36$.

The item difficulty index has a range of .00 to 1.00. An item whose $p = .00$ is one that no examinee answers correctly, and an item with $p = 1.00$ is one that all examinees answer correctly. The lower bound for an acceptable value of p depends on the number of options per item (k) and the number of examinees; a suggested formula for computing this lower bound is $[1 + 1.645\sqrt{(k - 1)/n}]/k$.

The optimum p value for an item depends on a number of factors, among them the purposes of the test and the number of response options. If the purpose of the test is to identify or select only a small percentage of the best students or applicants, then the test should be fairly difficult and have a low mean p value. If the test is designed to screen out only a few very poor students or candidates, then a high mean p is best.

The optimum mean p values corresponding to selected values of k, the number of response options, are given in Table 4–1. Acceptable item difficulty

TABLE 4–1 Optimum Mean Item Difficulty Index for Test Items with Various Numbers of Options

Number of options (k)	*Optimum mean difficulty index ($\bar{p}$)*
2	.85
3	.77
4	.74
5	.69
Open-ended (essay, short answer)	.50

Source: According to Lord (1952).

indexes will fall within a fairly narrow range, say ± .20 around these values. Although several very easy and several very difficult items are often included in a test, they actually add very little to the overall effectiveness of the test in differentiating among examinees possessing different amounts of knowledge or understanding of the test material.

The item discrimination index (*D*) is a measure of the effectiveness of an item in discriminating between high and low scorers on the test as a whole. The higher the value of *D* is, the more effective is the item. When *D* is 1.00, all examinees in the upper group and none of those in the lower group answered the item correctly. Rarely, however, is *D* equal to 1.00, and an item is usually considered acceptable if its *D* index is .30 or higher. *D* and *p* are, however, not independent indexes, and the minimum acceptable value of *D* varies with the value of *p*. A value of *D* somewhat smaller than .30 is acceptable as *p* becomes increasingly higher or lower than the optimum mean value, particularly when the sizes of the upper and lower comparison groups are large (Aiken, 1979b). Furthermore, an item having a low *D* index is not automatically discarded; it may be possible to save the item by modifying it. Good items are time-consuming to construct, so defective items should be revised if possible.

Group Differences and Speeded Tests

The results of an item analysis often vary substantially with the specific group that is tested, especially when the number of examinees is small. Certain items may be answered differently by males than females, by one ethnic group than another, by one socioeconomic group than another. In constructing a standardized test, it has become common practice to examine each item and its associated statistics for indications of group discrimination or bias. When test items are answered differently by one group than another, however, it does not necessarily mean that the items are biased against one of the groups. An item is biased, in a technical sense, only when it measures something different—a different characteristic or trait—in one group than in another. If item scores reflect true differences in whatever ability or trait the item was designed to measure, the item is not biased in this sense.

Problems also occur in the item analysis of speeded tests, on which the time limits are short and not all examinees have time to finish. On a speeded test, items placed near the end of the test are attempted by relatively few examinees. If those who reach and therefore attempt an item are the most able examinees, then the discrimination index (*D*) will probably be greater than it would be if the test time limits were ample. On the other hand, if the most careless responders are more likely to reach and attempt items toward the end of the test, then the *D* values of those items will tend to be smaller than the *D* values of items toward the beginning of the test. Various procedures have been suggested to take care of the problems encountered in analyzing items toward the end of speeded tests, but none is completely satisfactory (see Anastasi, 1982, pp. 215–217).

Conditions of testing other than time limits can affect the item easiness and discrimination indexes. Nevertheless, these two indexes provide useful information on the functioning of individual items. In general, it has been found that item analyses can result in significant improvements in test effectiveness (Bodner, 1980). The item discrimination index in particular is a fairly good measure of item quality (Pyrczak, 1973). Along with the difficulty index (p), D serves as a warning that something is wrong with an item. Consequently, these two indexes, together with the nature and size of the group tested, should be recorded on the back of a card containing the item. In this way a library of test items can be compiled for use in constructing future tests.

Internal Consistency versus Validity

The concept of item validity usually refers to the relationship of the item to an external criterion. But D is a measure of the relationship of the item to total test score rather than an external criterion. Therefore, selecting items with high D values for the final test produces an internally consistent test in which the correlations among items are highly positive. But an internally consistent test does not necessarily correlate highly with an external criterion. To construct a test that is highly correlated with an external criterion, one should choose items having low correlations with each other but high correlations with the criterion. Thus, selecting items on the basis of the D statistic will result in a different kind of test from selecting them on the basis of the item-criterion correlations. Which of these procedures is better depends on the purposes of the test constructor. If an internally consistent measure of a characteristic is desired, the item discrimination index will be used; if the most valid predictor of a particular external criterion is wanted, the item-criterion correlations will be used. Sometimes a combination of the two approaches is employed: a composite test is constructed from subtests having low correlations with each other and substantial correlations with an external criterion, but the items within each subtest are highly intercorrelated.

Criterion-Referenced Test Items

Difficulty and discrimination indexes may also be computed on criterion-referenced test items. In this case, the examinees are divided into two groups: an upper group consisting of the U examinees whose total test scores meet the criterion of mastery and a lower group consisting of the L examinees whose total test scores fail to meet the criterion. For a particular item, U_p is the number in the upper group who pass the item, and L_p is the number in the lower group who pass it. Then the item difficulty index is defined by formula 4.2. Because U and L are not necessarily equal, the item discrimination index is defined as

$$D = \frac{U_p}{U} - \frac{L_p}{L}. \qquad (4.4)$$

An external criterion may also be used in forming the upper and lower groups. In the case of a criterion-referenced achievement test, for example, examinees can be sorted into two groups: those who have received instruction in the subject matter associated with the test (*U*) and those who have received no such instruction (*L*). The *U* and *L* groups may also consist of the same individuals, both before (*L*) and after (*U*) instruction. In either case, formula 4.4 can be used to compute the item discrimination index (see Popham, 1981, pp. 300–303).

Analysis of Item Distracters

The analysis of multiple-choice items typically begins with the computation of a difficulty and a discrimination index for every item. A second analysis is concerned with the functioning of the *k*-1 distracters for each item. The algebraic sign and magnitude of the item discrimination index (*D*) provide some information on the functioning of the distracters as a whole. A positive *D* value means that examinees in the upper group tended to select the correct answer, while examinees in the lower group tended to select the distracters; the magnitude of *D* indicates the degree of this tendency. On the other hand, if *D* is negative, this means that the distracters as a whole were selected more frequently by the upper group than the lower group of examinees and that the item needs revising. The sign and magnitude of *D*, however, do not indicate whether all distracters are functioning similarly.

The simplest method of determining whether all distracters are working properly is to count the number of times that each distracter is selected as the right answer by examinees in the upper group and examinees in the lower group. If, on an otherwise satisfactory item, too many examinees in the upper group or too few of those in the lower group select a given distracter as the right answer, another distracter should be constructed. Because all distracters should be equally plausible to examinees who do not know the correct answer, every distracter on a specific item should also be selected by approximately the same number of examinees.

Item-Response Models

The approach to item analysis described above might be termed *simple item analysis* in that the procedure is fairly straightforward and, for the most part, easily performed by classroom teachers. At a somewhat more complex level is an item-analysis method which begins with the construction of a response curve for each item. In preparing an *item-response curve,* the proportion of examinees who get the item right is plotted against an internal criterion (for example, score on the entire test) or an external criterion of performance. Once the response curve is drawn, a difficulty level and a discriminative index can be computed for each item. The difficulty level (*b*) is the criterion score at which 50 percent of the examinees pass the item, and the discriminative index (*a*) is the slope of the item-response curve. Observe in the two item-response curves of Figure 4–1 that item A has a lower difficulty level but a steeper slope, and hence a greater discriminative index, than item B.[2] The similarity of these two indexes to the *p* and *D* values of simple item analysis is obvious. An item-response curve, however, goes further than a simple item analysis in providing a detailed picture of the functional relationship between the percentage passing the item and scores on the criterion measure.

In an extension of the item-response approach, item-response curves are constructed by plotting the percentage passing an item against estimates of examinee ability derived from a specified mathematical function (see Hulin, Drasgow & Parsons, 1983). Referred to as *latent trait theory, item characteristic curve theory* (ICC), or the *Rasch model*—depending on the assumptions and estimation procedures prescribed by the approach—these item-analysis methods relate examinees' performances on test items (percentage passing) to their estimated standings on a hypothetical latent ability trait or continuum. Because a thorough understanding of how these item-analysis models operate requires a fairly sophisticated background in mathematics, the technical details of the models will not be described here. As we shall see later in the chapter, however, item-response theories provide not only a new approach to item analysis but also techniques for constructing tests having certain specified characteristics.

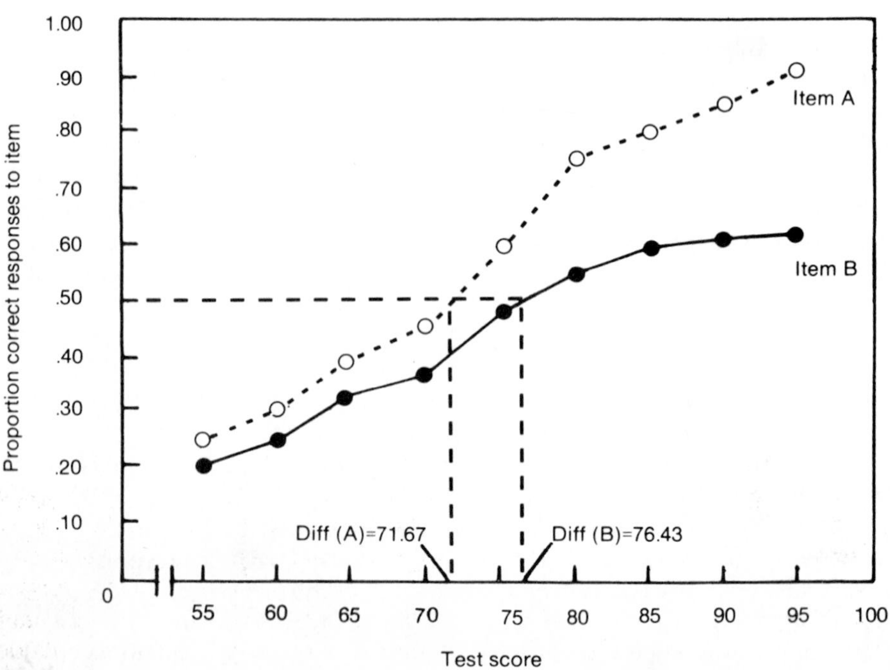

FIGURE 4–1 Illustrative item characteristic curves.
See text for explanation.

TEST STANDARDIZATION AND NORMS

Item analyses should be conducted on all newly constructed tests, whether teacher made or standardized. In addition, keeping a record of the performances of classes of students or other groups of examinees can provide a frame of reference for interpreting scores on both teacher-made and standardized tests. It is with standardized tests, however, that the greatest attention and effort are directed toward collecting scores from large groups of individuals and converting the scores to test norms.

Standardized Tests

For a test to be standardized, it must be administered with standard directions under uniform conditions to a sample of examinees who are representative of the population for which the test is intended. The major purpose of the standardization procedure is to determine the distribution of raw scores in the standardization group *(norm group)*. The obtained raw scores are then converted to some form of derived scores, or *norms*—age equivalents, grade equivalents, percentile ranks, or standard scores. Most test manuals contain tables of norms listing the converted score equivalents of particular raw scores. Examinees' standings on a test may be evaluated by referring their raw scores to the norm table appropriate for their particular group. In this way, norms serve as a frame of reference for interpreting raw scores; they indicate an examinee's standing on the test relative to the distribution of scores obtained by other people of the same age, grade, sex, and so on.

In terms of sample size and representativeness, group tests, and achievement tests in particular, are usually more adequately standardized than individual tests. Norms for group tests are frequently based on as many as 100,000 people, whereas the size of the norm group for a carefully standardized individual test is more likely to be around 2,000 to 4,000.

Selecting a Norm Group

To serve effectively in the interpretation of test scores, norms must be appropriate to the group or individual being evaluated. For example, a particular fourth-grader's score may surpass that of 80 percent of fourth-grade children and 60 percent of sixth-graders. Although it may be of some interest to compare this student's test score with those of the third- and sixth-grade norm groups, of primary concern is the student's standing in the fourth-grade group. Whenever a person's raw score is converted by referring to a table of norms, it is important to note the nature (age, sex, ethnic group, educational and socioeconomic status, geographical region, and so on) of the particular norm group and to include this information in all communications regarding that person's test performance. Another important factor to consider is when the norms were obtained. During times of rapid social and educational change, the norms on certain tests can quickly become outdated. For example, changes in school curricula may necessitate restandardization and perhaps modifying or reconstructing an achievement test every five or ten years.

When standardizing a test for the purpose of determining norms, the population of people for whom the test is intended (the *target population*) should be carefully defined. Then a representative sample of the target population is selected as the test standardization sample. The manner in which the standardization sample is selected varies from simple random sampling to more complex sampling strategies such as stratified random sampling and cluster sampling. In *simple random sampling,* every person in the population has an equal chance of being selected as part of the sample. *Stratified random sampling* consists of stratifying, or classifying, the target population on certain variables (for example, age, grade level, sex) and then selecting an appropriate percentage of people at random from each stratum. Because there is less chance of selecting an atypical, or biased, sample when the stratified procedure is used, the obtained norms provide a sounder basis for interpreting scores on the test than do norms obtained by simple random sampling.

Somewhat more economical than stratified random sampling and more likely than random sampling to provide a representative sample of the target population is cluster sampling. *Cluster sampling* begins by dividing a designated population of schools or other relevant units into areas or clusters. The next step is to select a specified proportion of the clusters at random and then to choose at random within each cluster a certain number of schools or other subunits. The final step is to test all students, or a randomly selected subset of them, within each school.

Administering all items on a test to a stratified random or cluster sample of people is tedious and time-consuming, so efforts have been made to devise less costly strategies for determining test norms. One such strategy is to sample test items. In *item sampling,* different randomly selected examinees answer different sets of items on the test. One group of examinees answers one set of items, and other groups answer other sets. In this way, it is possible to administer more items to a large sample of people in a fixed period of time. The results can then be combined to conduct item analyses and determine norms for representative samples of examinees on a wide range of content. Research employing Lord's (1962) item-sampling model has shown that the resulting norms are quite similar to those obtained by the traditional but more laborious process of administering the entire test to a large representative sample of individuals (e.g., Owens & Stufflebeam, 1969).

Types of Norms

Figure 4–2, a report of the scores of a student who took the Gates-MacGinitie Reading Tests, illustrates several types of norms: national and local percentile ranks, national and local stanines, grade equivalents (grade norms), and standard

SCORES FOR THE
Gates-MacGinitie Reading Tests
Second Edition
LEVEL: D FORM: 1

TEACHER: MISS BETH YATES
BUILDING: LINCOLN ELEM
SCHOOL/DISTRICT: NORTH CENTRAL
OTHER INFORMATION:

THIS REPORT PREPARED FOR:
RACHEL GRIFFITH

DATE OF BIRTH: JUNE (MONTH) 1972 (YEAR)
GRADE: 5
DATE OF TESTING: NOV. 1982
SEX: FEMALE

PROCESS NUMBER: 000-0328-000

TYPES OF SCORES	SCORES		
	Vocabulary	Comprehension	Total
NUMBER OF ITEMS ATTEMPTED	45	43	88
RAW SCORES	33	36	69
NORMAL CURVE EQ. (NCE)	66	80	74
NAT'L. PERCENTILE RANK (PR)	78	92	87
STANINE (S)	7	8	7
GRADE EQUIVALENT (GE)	6.7	9.7	7.7
EXT'D. SCALE SCORE (ESS)	538	594	560

PLOTTED NATIONAL STANINE BAND

TEST AREA	1 2 3 4 5 6 7 8 9 (AVERAGE)
Vocabulary	XXX
Comprehension	XXX
Total	XXX

MORE ABOUT THIS STANINE BAND:

This stanine band is plotted in such a manner as to readily determine if the bands overlap. If the bands do overlap, there is no meaningful difference between the test scores. However, if the bands do not overlap, there is a meaningful difference in the scores.

MORE ABOUT THE SCORES:
A MESSAGE ABOUT RACHEL'S READING SCORES

RACHEL'S OVERALL READING DEVELOPMENT IS BEST SHOWN IN THE NATIONAL PERCENTILE RANK FOR HER TOTAL SCORE. RACHEL'S PERCENTILE RANK OF 87 MEANS THAT SHE SCORED BETTER THAN 87% OF FIFTH GRADERS NATIONALLY AND THAT 13% SCORED AS WELL AS OR BETTER THAN SHE DID. SO RACHEL'S READING ACHIEVEMENT IS ABOVE AVERAGE FOR HER GRADE.

PREPARED BY RIVERSIDE SCORING SERVICE

9-80400

FIGURE 4–2 Individual Student Score Report, Gates-MacGinitie Reading Tests, Second Edition.

(Reproduced from Gates-MacGinitie Reading Tests, Second Edition, Copyright © 1978, with permission of the Publisher, The Riverside Publishing Company, 8420 W. Bryn Mawr Avenue, Chicago, IL 60631. All rights reserved.)

scores. Among the norms not shown in this report form are age equivalents (age norms) and certain types of standard score norms. The meanings of the various types of norms will be discussed in this section.

National, Regional, and Local Norms The norms published in test manuals are useful in comparing an examinee's score with those of a sample of people from various localities, sometimes a cross-section of the entire nation. But a test administrator is typically more interested in determining how well an examinee has done in comparison with the other students in the school, school system, state, or region rather than compared to a nationally selected sample. When interest is restricted to the test scores of a particular school, the test administrator will want to convert raw test scores to *local norms* by the procedures discussed below. Local norms are used quite often for selection and placement purposes in schools and colleges.

Age and Grade Norms Among the most popular types of norms, primarily because they are easily understood by test users, are age norms and grade norms. An *age norm* (age equivalent, educational age) is the median score on a test obtained by children of a given chronological age; a *grade norm* (grade equivalent) is the median score obtained by children at a given grade level. Age norms are expressed in years and twelve one-month intervals. For the fifth year, for example, age norms range from 5–0 to 5–11, or 5 years, 0 months to 5 years, 11 months. Grade norms are expressed in ten one-month intervals, the assumption being that growth during the summer months on the characteristic of interest is inconsequential. For example, the range of grade norms for the fifth grade is 5–0 to 5–9, in one-month intervals from the first to the last month of the school year.

Despite their popularity, age and grade norms have serious shortcomings, the main one being that growth in psychological and educational characteristics is not uniform over the entire range of ages or grades. Thus, a difference of two months' growth in achievement at grade five (say from 5–2 to 5–4) is not educationally equivalent to two months' growth in achievement at a later grade level (say from 8–2 to 8–4). Actually, the age and grade units become progressively smaller with an increase in age or grade. Since age and grade norms incorrectly imply that the rate of increase in tested abilities is constant from year to year, their use is frequently discouraged by educational measurement specialists. Norms in which the unit of measurement is more nearly constant are preferred.

Because of their convenience, age and grade norms continue to be used at the elementary school level, where the assumption of equal growth units is less seriously violated. Even at this level, however, age and grade norms should be supplemented with the percentile or standard score norms for a particular age or grade.

Modal Age Norms Typically, the students in a given grade on whom grade norms are determined have a rather wide range of ages; the scores of certain students who are actually much older (or younger) than the average student in that grade are included in the norms. To provide a more accurate index of the average score of students at a given grade level, the scores of those students who are much older or much younger are sometimes omitted and the median score computed only on students who are of the appropriate age for that grade. These "restricted" grade norms are referred to as *modal age norms.* Modal age norms, which are found infrequently in current achievement test manuals, are mentioned here primarily for their historical interest.

Mental Age Norms The term *mental age* will be recalled from the brief discussion in Chapter 1 of the history of mental measurement. This concept, introduced by Alfred Binet, is a type of age norm employed on various intelligence tests. The mental age score of a particular examinee corresponds to the chronological age of that subgroup of children (all of the same chronological age) in the standardization group whose median score on the test was the same as that of the examinee. It has been the practice in many special schools for the mentally retarded to group children according to their mental ages, rather than their chronological ages, for purposes of instruction.

Quotients An older practice in testing, which has virtually disappeared, is to convert an examinee's age norm to a quotient by dividing the age score by the person's chronological age and multiplying the result by 100. Thus, the *intelligence quotient (ratio IQ)* on the older Stanford-Binet Intelligence Scale was defined as

$$IQ = 100(MA/CA), \tag{4.5}$$

where MA is the examinee's mental age and CA the chronological age in months. Similarly, an *educational quotient* on certain achievement tests was computed as the ratio of educational age (age norm on an educational achievement test) to chronological age. Occasionally, an *accomplishment quotient* was computed (by combining the results of an intelligence test with those of an educational achievement test) as the ratio of educational age to mental age. Some of these quotients, particularly the IQ, are still used as test norms, but the practice is discouraged by authorities in psychological measurement.

Percentile Norms Percentile norms consist of a table of percentages corresponding to particular raw scores. The raw scores are referred to as *percentiles,* and the percentage of the norm group falling below a particular score is the *percentile rank* of that score. For example, referring to columns 2 and 5 of the distribution in Table 4–2, the percentile rank of a score of 775 is approximately 99, and the percentile rank of a score of 475 is approximately 23. Or one may say that the 99th percentile for these data is 775, and the 23rd percentile is 475.

Because percentile norms are often needed for selection and placement purposes in a given school or grade group, the procedure for computing them will be described in some detail. Columns 1 and 3 of Table 4–2 represent a frequency distribution of 250 scores on a scholastic aptitude test, and column 2 gives the midpoints of the score intervals. To compute the entry in column 4 (cumulative frequency below midpoint) for a particular interval, the frequencies on all intervals up to that interval are summed. To this sum is added one-half of the frequency on that interval. For example, the entry 227.0 for the interval 650–699 is computed as $(1 + 13 + 25 + 38 + 65 + 49 + 27) + \frac{1}{2}(18) =$

TABLE 4–2 Percentile Ranks and Standard Scores Corresponding to Midpoints of a Test Score Distribution

(1) Score interval	(2) Midpoint	(3) Frequency	(4) Cumulative frequency below midpoint	(5) Percentile rank	(6) z	(7) Z	(8) z_n	(9) T
750–799	774.5	3	248.5	99.4(99)	2.59	76	2.51	75
700–749	724.5	11	241.5	96.6(97)	2.03	70	1.83	68
650–699	674.5	18	227.0	90.8(91)	1.48	65	1.33	63
600–649	624.5	27	204.5	81.8(82)	0.92	59	0.91	59
550–599	574.5	49	166.5	66.6(67)	0.37	54	0.43	54
500–549	524.5	65	109.5	43.8(44)	−0.19	48	−0.16	48
450–499	474.5	38	58.0	23.2(23)	−0.74	43	−0.73	43
400–449	424.5	25	26.5	10.6(11)	−1.30	37	−1.25	37
350–399	374.5	13	7.5	3.0(3)	−1.86	31	−1.88	31
300–349	324.5	1	0.5	0.2(0)	−2.41	26	−2.88	21

227.0. Since the entry for a particular interval in column 4 is the cumulative frequency below the midpoint of that interval, the percentile rank of a given interval midpoint may be computed by dividing the respective number in column 4 by n, the total number of scores. For the data in Table 4–2, $n = 250$, so each of the percentile ranks in column 5 is determined by dividing the respective cumulative frequency in column 4 by 250, multiplying the result by 100, and rounding off to the nearest whole number. For example, the percentile rank of the midpoint 674.5 is $100(227/250) = 90.8 \approx 91$.

Percentile norms are easy to compute and to understand; therefore they are quite common in published tests. Tables of percentile norms within grades, ages, sex, occupations, and other groups are reported for many cognitive and affective tests. Unfortunately, the problem of unequal score units, which was referred to previously in the discussion of age and grade norms, is not solved by percentile norms. As may be observed graphically on the scale labeled "Percentile Equivalents" in Figure 4–3, percentile rank units are not equal on all parts of the scale. Percentile ranks are ordinal-level rather than interval-level measures. Notice, for example, that the distance between the percentile ranks 5 and 10 (or 90 and 95) on the Percentile Equivalents scale of Figure 4–3 is larger than the distance between 40 and 45 (or 60 and 65). Although the numerical differences between the ranks are the same, the size of the percentile rank unit becomes progressively smaller toward the center of the scale.

The tendency of percentile rank units to bunch up in the middle and spread out at the extremes of the scale causes difficulty in the interpretation of changes and differences in percentile norms. Thus, the difference in achievement between a person whose percentile rank on an achievement test is 5 and one whose percentile rank is 10 is not equal to the difference in achievement between a person whose percentile rank is 40 and one whose percentile rank is 45. On

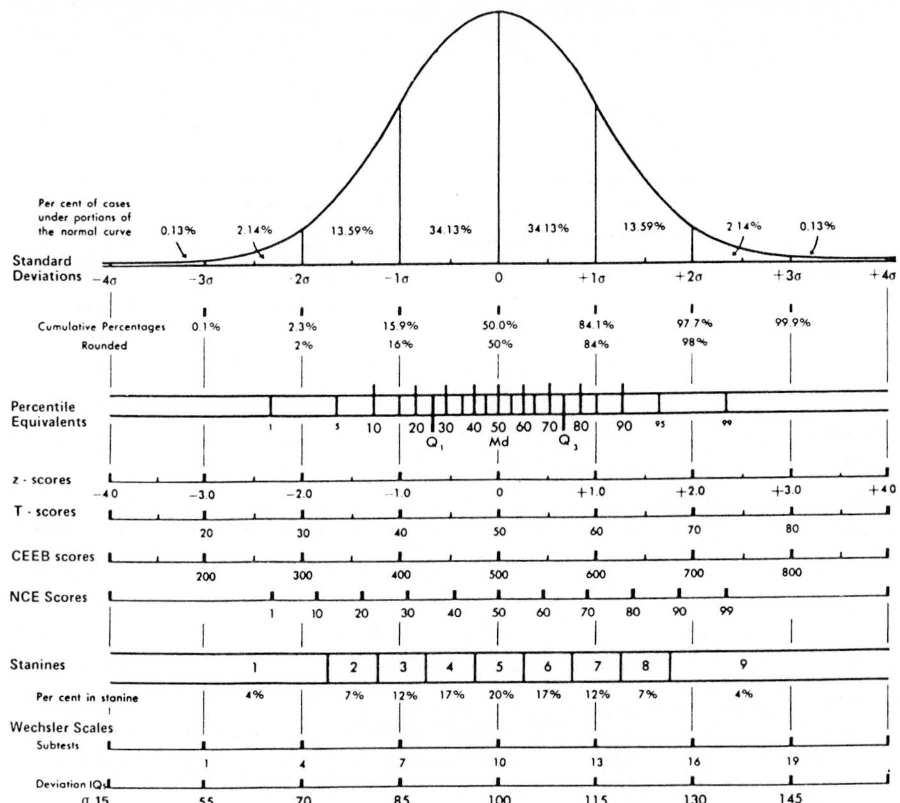

Percentile Ranks and Standard Scores Corresponding to Various Points on the Baseline of a Normal Distribution of Scores. **FIGURE 4–3**
(H. G. Seashore, *Methods of expressing test scores,* The Psychological Corporation Test Service Bulletin, No. 48, 1955.)

the percentile rank scale, 10–5 is greater than 45–40, because the unit of measurement for the first difference is larger. With practice, however, it is not difficult to interpret percentile norms. One must simply remember to give greater weight to percentile rank differences at the extremes of the scale than to those toward the center.

Standard Score Norms Unlike percentile ranks, standard scores represent measurements on an interval scale. *Standard score norms* are converted scores having any desired mean and standard deviation. There are many different types of standard scores: *z* scores, *Z* scores, CEEB scores, deviation IQ scores, stanine scores, and *T* scores. Basically, all are transformations of *z* scores.

z Scores The *z* score equivalents of a particular distribution of raw scores may be determined by the following formula:

$$z = \frac{X - \overline{X}}{s}, \tag{4.6}$$

where X is a given raw score, $\overline{X}$ the arithmetic mean, and s the standard deviation of the distribution of scores. Transforming the distribution of raw scores to z scores results in a new distribution having the same shape but a different mean and standard deviation from those of the raw score distribution. The mean of z scores is 0, and the standard deviation is 1. The z scores corresponding to the interval midpoints listed in column 2 are given in column 6 of Table 4–2. It may be determined by procedures described in Chapter 1 that the mean and standard deviation of the distribution of scores in Table 4–2 are 541.50 and 90.30, respectively. Therefore, the z score corresponding to the midpoint 774.5 is $(774.5 - 541.5)/90.3 = 2.58$. The z scores of the other midpoints may be found in the same way. On the first line under "Typical Standard Scores" in Figure 4–3 are the z scores corresponding to various points along the baseline of the normal curve.

Z Scores The fact that z scores can be negative or positive decimal numbers creates some difficulty in manipulating the scores. This problem can be solved by multiplying the z scores by a constant and adding another constant to the products. If the z scores are multiplied by 10, and 50 is added to the products, a new set of scores, *Z scores,* having a mean of 50 and a standard deviation of 10, is produced. The new distribution of Z scores also has the same shape as the original raw score distribution; only the mean and standard deviation have been changed (see column 7 of Table 4–2).

CEEB Scores Instead of having a mean of 50 and a standard deviation of 10, the scores on the two sections (Verbal and Mathematical) of the College Entrance Examination Board's Scholastic Aptitude Test (SAT) were originally transformed by multiplying the corresponding z scores by 100 and adding 500 to the result. This was done to the results of the tests administered in 1941, giving a new score distribution having a mean of 500 and a standard deviation of 100. The scores that examinees obtain on the SAT now administered, however, are not transformed each year to give a mean of 500 and a standard deviation of 100. Rather, in order to have a constant score unit for comparing test results from year to year, since 1941 the scale of SAT scores has been based on the results of the 1941 testing.

AGCT and Wechsler Scores The score scale on the Army General Classification Test (AGCT), which was formerly employed in the selection and placement of soldiers, had a mean of 100 and a standard deviation of 20. In contrast, raw scores on the subtests of the Wechsler intelligence scales were transformed to have a mean of 10 and a standard deviation of 3, while the total scores of the norm groups on the Wechsler scales were converted to have a mean of 100 and a standard deviation of 15 (see last two lines of Figure 4–3).

Normalized Standard Scores All of the standard score norms referred to above are simple linear transformations of raw scores; the distribution of converted scores has a different mean and standard deviation from the raw score distribution, but the shapes of the two distributions are identical. If the raw score distribution is asymmetrical, the converted score distribution also will be asymmetrical.

In order to make the scores from different tests more directly comparable, there is a transformation procedure that not only affects the mean and standard deviation but also changes the shape of the distribution of raw scores to that of a normal distribution. The conversion of a group of raw scores to *normalized standard scores* begins with the computation of the percentile ranks of the raw scores. Then, from a table of areas under the normal curve (Appendix B), the z score corresponding to each percentile rank is found. For example, assume that the midpoints (column 2) of the distribution in Table 4–2 are to be converted to normalized standard scores. Since the percentile ranks of these midpoints have already been computed (column 5), all that needs to be done is to convert the percentile ranks to proportions (for example, 99.4 becomes .994). Then, from the table in Appendix B, the z scores below which the given proportions of the area lie may be determined. Thus, the z score (z_n) below which .994 of the area under a normal curve lies is 2.51. The other normalized z scores in column 8 of Table 4–2 were determined in the same manner. To get rid of decimals and negative numbers, these z_n scores were transformed to T scores by the formula $T = 10z_n + 50$ (column 9). The new normal distribution of T scores has a mean of 50 and a standard deviation of 10.

The z_n scores may be transformed to normalized scores having any desired mean and standard deviation. One popular scale, which has been used extensively on tests constructed for the U.S. Air Force and for grading purposes in certain educational institutions, is the stanine ("standard nine") scale. The *stanine scale,* a normalized standard score scale with a mean of 5 and a standard deviation of approximately 2, is represented by the third scale from the bottom in Figure 4–3. There are nine different ranges, or stanines, on the scale. These ranges are represented by the numbers 1 through 9, and, as shown in the figure, a certain percentage of the examinees falls in each stanine group. The stanine scale, however, is not a true standard score scale because the first and ninth stanines are open-ended. Notice in Figure 4–3 that the widths of stanines 2 through 8 are equal, indicating equal standard score units, but that stanines 1 and 9 are much wider than the others. One advantage of stanine scores is that they represent ranges rather than specific points. This helps combat the tendency to view test scores as precise, unvarying measures of individual differences. Another procedure having the same effect is to report not only the percentile rank or standard score corresponding to a given raw score but also a percentile rank or standard score interval within which the examinee's true standing on the test might reasonably be expected to fall. This practice is a recognition of the fact that scores on psychological and educational tests are not exact measurements but are subject to errors of measurement, a topic discussed in more detail in Chapter 5.

Parallel, Equated, and Comparable Tests

There are many situations, involving research with or applications of psychological and educational tests, in which more than one form of a test is needed. Such equivalent, or *parallel,* tests are, understandably, rather expensive and time-consuming to construct. Traditionally this has been accomplished by constructing two tests having the same number and kinds of items and that, when administered to the same examinees, yield equal means and standard deviations. The resulting parallel forms are then "equated" by converting the scores on one form of the test to the same units as the other form. This may be done, for example, by the *equipercentile method* of changing the scores on each test form to percentile ranks. Then a table of equivalent scores on the two forms is constructed by equating the score at the *p*th percentile on the first form to the score at the *p*th percentile on the second.

Tests may also be equated, or rather made comparable, by "anchoring" the tests to a common test or pool of items, as has been done in the case of the Scholastic Aptitude Test (SAT). By using a set of common anchor items on each new form that are the same as a subset of the items used on at least one earlier form of the test, scores on the new form of the SAT administered each year are equated to at least one previous form—going all the way back to the form administered to the 1941 standardization sample.

Item-response models were referred to previously under item analysis and norms. These approaches, which prescribe methods of calibrating a set of test items on latent traits or item characteristic curves, have also been used to equate tests. The procedures are economical in that item sampling, in which randomly selected subsets of items are administered to different randomly selected groups of people, is employed. But whatever the method of trying to equate tests may be—equipercentile, item response, linear or nonlinear score transformations—test forms having different reliabilities cannot be strictly equated. Similarly, tests that measure different abilities or other psychological characteristics cannot be equated in the strict sense of the term. In both cases, the best that can be done is to make the tests "comparable" (American Educational Research Association et al., 1985).

SUMMARY

The major purpose of an item analysis is to improve a test by revising or discarding ineffective items. Item analysis also provides specific information on what examinees know and do not know.

Test items may be analyzed by comparing item responses with scores on an external criterion (such as teacher-assigned marks or supervisors' ratings) or an internal criterion (for example, total test scores). If the goal of the test constructor is to produce a test that is most predictive of scores on an external criterion, then the items should be validated against total test scores.

Various statistics (point-biserial coefficient, *D*, and others) may be used to validate test items against internal or external criteria. These coefficients, which are indexes of the relationship between dichotomously scored (right = 1, wrong = 0) items and scores on the criterion, provide a basis for accepting or rejecting specific items.

Two simple indexes that may be computed in the item analysis of a teacher-made test are the item difficulty index (p) and the item discrimination index (D). These indexes are applicable to norm-referenced and criterion-referenced tests. The optimum value of p depends on the purposes of the test and the number of options per item; intermediate values are preferable to very high or very low values. In most situations a D value of .30 or higher is required to accept an item.

In addition to computing their difficulty and discrimination indexes, test items should be examined for signs of bias, ambiguity, and the effects of speededness. The frequency distribution of responses to the k-1 distracters on an item should also be determined, separately for the upper and lower criterion groups, to detect marked variations from uniformity and consequently poorly functioning distracters.

Item-response models plot percentage passing on each item against total test scores or against mathematically derived estimates of ability. The difficulty level and discriminative index for an item are determined from the resulting item-response curve. Various item-response models, including latent trait theory, item characteristic curve theory, and the Rasch model, have been proposed.

In standardizing a test, it should be administered to a representative sample of people under standard (uniform) conditions. Norms computed from the obtained test scores provide a frame of reference for interpreting scores made by people who subsequently take the test. Test norms have traditionally been determined by testing a sample (random, stratified random, cluster) of the population of people for whom the test is intended. Less expensive and more efficient than traditional test-standardization procedures are item-sampling techniques in which not only people but also test items are sampled, different groups of examinees answering different sets of items.

Test norms may be computed on national, regional, or local samples, depending on the purposes and resources of the test users. Age and grade norms, which are determined most often for tests of achievement, permit comparing an individual's test score with the average score of children at a certain age or grade level. The main shortcoming of age and grade norms is that growth in achievement or ability is not uniform over age or grade levels. Percentile norms, in which a raw test score is converted to the percentage of examinees in the standardization group who made that score or lower, also suffer from the problem of unequal score units. However, age, grade, and percentile norms are all easily understood and convenient to use, so they will undoubtedly continue to be popular.

Standard score norms are converted scores having a designated mean and standard deviation. Unlike the ordinal measurement represented by age, grade, and percentile norms, standard scores (z, T, CEEB, and others) are interval-level measures. Not all standard scores are normally distributed, but they can be transformed to be normal (such as stanine scores).

Scores on parallel tests may be scaled to achieve comparability, if not strictly equated, in various ways. Tests have traditionally been equated by the equipercentile method, but more recent approaches entail applications of item-response models.

EXERCISES

1. What are the difficulty (p) and discrimination (D) indexes of a test item administered to 75 people if 18 of the upper group (upper 27 percent on total test score) and 12 of the lower group (lower 27 percent on total test score) get the item right? Note that, rounding off, there are 20 people in the upper group and 20 people in the lower group.
2. Compute the difficulty (p) and discrimination (D) indexes for an item on a criterion-referenced test taken by 50 people, 30 of whom reach the criterion level on total test score. Of the 30 who reach the criterion level on the test, 20 get the item right; of the 20 who do not reach the criterion level, 10 get the item right.
3. The following two-way table indicates whether each of 20 examinees got each of the ten items on a four-option multiple-choice test right (r), wrong (w), or did not answer it (b). Total test scores of the examinees are given on the last line of the table. Classifying examinees A through J in the upper group (U) and examinees K through T in the lower group (L), compute the difficulty index (p) and the discrimination index (D) for each item. Write these values on the last two columns of the table. Inspect the p and D indexes to decide which items are acceptable and which items need revising or discarding.

	Examinee																					
Item	*A*	*B*	*C*	*D*	*E*	*F*	*G*	*H*	*I*	*J*	*K*	*L*	*M*	*N*	*O*	*P*	*Q*	*R*	*S*	*T*	*p*	*D*
1	r	r	r	w	w	w	r	r	r	r	w	r	r	w	w	w	r	w	w	w		
2	r	r	w	r	w	r	w	r	w	r	r	w	w	r	w	w	w	w	r	w		
3	r	w	r	r	r	w	r	w	r	w	w	r	r	w	w	r	w	w	w	w		
4	r	r	r	r	r	r	w	r	w	r	r	w	w	r	r	w	w	w	w	w		
5	r	r	w	r	r	r	r	r	w	w	w	r	w	w	w	w	w	w	w	w		
6	r	r	r	r	r	r	w	r	r	r	r	w	r	r	w	r	w	r	w	r		
7	r	w	w	w	r	r	r	r	w	r	w	w	r	w	r	w	w	r	r	w		
8	r	r	r	r	r	w	w	w	r	w	r	r	w	w	w	r	r	w	w	w		
9	r	r	r	r	w	r	r	w	r	r	r	r	w	r	r	w	w	w	w	w		
10	r	r	r	w	r	r	r	w	r	w	w	w	w	w	w	w	r	w	w	w		
Score	10	8	7	7	7	7	6	6	6	6	5	5	4	4	3	3	3	2	2	1		

4. Suppose that George makes a raw score of 65 on an arithmetic test having a mean of 50 and a standard deviation of 10, but he makes a raw score of 80 on a reading test having a mean of 75 and a standard deviation of 15.

What are George's z scores and Z scores on the two tests? Is he better in arithmetic or reading?

5. By referring to the normal curve table in Appendix B, find the z scores corresponding to the 10th, 20th, 30th, 40th, 50th, 60th, 70th, 80th, and 90th percentile ranks. Then convert the resulting z scores to T scores, CEEB scores, stanines, and deviation IQs.
6. Using Table 4–2 as a model, construct a frequency distribution of the thirty scores listed below (let $i = 3$). Compute the percentile rank, z, Z, z_n, and T scores corresponding to the interval midpoints:

82	85	70	91	75	88	78	82	95
79	86	90	87	77	87	73	80	96
86	81	85	93	84	89	92	89	84
83	79	74						

7. Why are standard score norms considered superior to age, grade, and percentile norms?
8. Under what conditions would it be useful to compute p and D using both internal and external criteria?

NOTES

1. Upper and lower halves are sometimes used when the number of examinees is small.
2. The difficulty levels of items A and B are, respectively, 71.67 and 76.43; the discriminative indexes (linear slopes) are, respectively, .0182 and .0116.

SUGGESTED READINGS

Baglin, R. F. (1981). Does "nationally" normed really mean nationally? *Journal of Educational Measurement, 18,* 97–107.

Barker, D., & Ebel, R. L. (1982, Jan.). Comparison of difficulty and discrimination values of selected true-false item types. *Contemporary Educational Psychology, 7,* 35–40.

Berk, R. A. (1980). Item analysis. In R. Berk (ed.), *Criterion-reference testing: State of the art.* Baltimore: Johns Hopkins University Press.

Ebel, R. L. (1979). How to improve test quality through item analysis. In *Essentials of educational measurement* (pp. 258–272). 3d ed. Englewood Cliffs, NJ: Prentice-Hall.

Green, K. (1984). Effects of item characteristics on multiple-choice item difficulty. *Educational and Psychological Measurement, 44,* 551–561.

Hulin, C. L., Drasgow, F., & Parsons, C. K. (1983). *Item response theory.* Homewood, IL: Dorsey.

Popham, W. J., & Lindheim, E. (1980). The practical side of criterion-referenced test development. *NCME Measurement in Education, 10*(4), 1–8.

Sumner, R. (1985). Test norms. In T. Husen & T. N. Postlethwaite (eds.), *International encyclopedia of education* (vol. 9, pp. 5205–5209). New York: Wiley.

Chapter 5

Reliability and Validity

Of major importance in constructing or selecting a test that will produce accurate, meaningful scores are the reliability and validity of the test. These two topics have received a great deal of professional attention from both a theoretical and a practical standpoint, and only brief consideration can be given here to some of the relevant concepts and issues. Although condensed, the material presented in this chapter should be a guide to understanding test manuals and evaluating specific tests and other assessment instruments.

RELIABILITY

To be useful, tests and other measuring instruments must be fairly consistent, or reliable, in what they measure. The concept of the *reliability* of a test refers to its relative freedom from unsystematic errors of measurement. A test is reliable if it measures consistently under varying conditions that can produce measurement errors. Unsystematic errors affecting test scores vary in a random, unpredictable manner from situation to situation; hence, they lower test reliability. On the other hand, systematic (constant) errors may inflate or deflate test scores, but they do so in a fixed way and hence do not affect the reliability of the test. Some of the variables on which unsystematic error depends are the particular sample of questions on the test, the conditions of administration, and the level of motivation or attentiveness of the examinee at testing time.

Reliability Theory

In classical test theory it is assumed that a person's observed score on a test is composed of a "true" score plus some unsystematic measurement error. A *true score* is defined as the average of the scores that would be obtained if a person took the test an infinite number of times. It should be emphasized that a person's true test score can never be measured exactly but must be estimated from his or her observed score. Classical test theory also assumes that the variance of observed scores (s^2_{obs}) for a group of examinees is equal to the variance of their true scores (s^2_{tru}) plus the variance of the unsystematic errors of measurement (s^2_{err}):

$$s^2_{obs} = s^2_{tru} + s^2_{err}. \tag{5.1}$$

Then test reliability (r_{11}) is defined as the ratio of true variance to observed variance, or the proportion of the observed variance accounted for by true variance:

$$r_{11} = \frac{s^2_{tru}}{s^2_{obs}}. \tag{5.2}$$

The proportion of observed variance accounted for by error variance (or unaccounted for by true variance) can be determined from formulas 5.1 and 5.2 to be

$$\frac{s^2_{err}}{s^2_{obs}} = 1 - r_{11}. \tag{5.3}$$

The reliability of a test is expressed as a positive decimal number ranging from .00 to 1.00, where $r_{11} = 1.00$ indicates perfect reliability and $r_{11} = .00$ the absence of reliability. Since the variance of true scores cannot be computed directly, test reliability is usually estimated by analyzing the effects of variations in administration conditions and test content on examinees' scores. It was noted that reliability is not affected by systematic changes in scores, which may occur because of learning or growth, but only by those unsystematic changes that have different effects on different examinees. Such unsystematic factors affect the error variance of the test, and hence its reliability. Each of the several methods of estimating test reliability—test-retest, parallel forms, and internal consistency—takes into account somewhat different conditions that may produce unsystematic changes in test scores and consequently affect the magnitude of the error variance.

Test-Retest and Parallel-Forms Coefficients

The most direct way of estimating a test's reliability is to administer the test to the same group of examinees on two occasions separated by an interval of several days or weeks. Then a *test-retest reliability coefficient* can be determined by computing the correlation between the scores on the two administrations. This procedure takes into account errors produced by differences in conditions associated with the two occasions on which the test is administered. Because the same test is administered on both occasions, error due to different samples of test items is not reflected in a test-retest coefficient.

In the *parallel-forms* procedure, two tests that are equivalent, in the sense that they contain the same kinds of items of equal difficulty but not the same items, are administered to the same examinees. Then the correlation between the two sets of test scores is computed. Unlike the test-retest procedure, the method of parallel forms takes into account error variance produced by using different samples of items. Perhaps the most desirable procedure for estimating reliability is to correlate the scores on a form of the test administered on one occasion with scores on a parallel form administered on a subsequent occasion. In this way, both errors due to different samples of items and errors due to different conditions of administration are taken into account.

Internal Consistency Coefficients

Although parallel forms are available for a number of tests, particularly cognitive tests, a parallel form is expensive and frequently difficult to construct. Therefore, a less direct method of assessing the effects of different samples of items on test reliability was devised—the method of internal consistency. Errors of measurement caused by different conditions or times of administration are, however, not reflected in an internal consistency coefficient. Therefore, internal consistency coefficients are not really equivalent to test-retest or parallel-forms coefficients.

Split-Half Method It is often convenient to view a single test as consisting of two parts (parallel forms), each of which measures the same thing. Thus, a test can be administered and separate scores assigned to every examinee on two arbitrarily selected halves of the test. For example, an examinee may be given one score on the odd-numbered items and a second score on the even-numbered items. Then the correlation (r_{oe}) between the two sets of scores is a parallel-forms reliability coefficient for a test half as long as the original test. Assuming that the two halves are equivalent (their means are equal and their variances the same), then the reliability of the whole test can be estimated by the Spearman-Brown prophecy formula:[1]

$$r_{11} = \frac{2r_{oe}}{1 + r_{oe}} \tag{5.4}$$

As a computational example of using the odd-even reliability formula, if the correlation of total scores on the odd-numbered items with total scores on the even-numbered items is .80, the estimated reliability of the whole test is $r_{11} = 2(.80)/(1 + .80) = .89$.

Kuder-Richardson Method Obviously there are many different ways of dividing a test into halves. Since each way yields a different value of r_{11}, it is not clear which halving procedure is best. One solution to the problem is to take the average of the reliability coefficients obtained from all possible half-splits as the best estimate of reliability. This could be done empirically, but even with a digital computer it would be a very time-consuming procedure. For example, with a test of only twenty items, one would have to compute and average 92,378 split-half reliability coefficients![2]

Under certain conditions the mean of all split-half coefficients can be estimated by one of the following formulas:

$$r_{11} = \frac{k}{k-1}\left[1 - \frac{\sum_{i=1}^{k} p_i(1-p_i)}{s^2}\right], \qquad (5.5)$$

$$r_{11} = \frac{k}{k-1}\left[1 - \frac{\bar{X}(k-\bar{X})}{ks^2}\right], \qquad (5.6)$$

where k is the number of items on the test, $\bar{X}$ the mean of total test scores, s^2 the variance of total test scores, and p_i the proportion of examinees getting item i correct; the products $p_i(1 - p_i)$ are summed over all k items.[3] Formula 5.5 is known as Kuder-Richardson (K-R) formula 20, and formula 5.6 is K-R formula 21. Unlike formula 5.5, in using formula 5.6 one assumes that all items are of equal difficulty. Furthermore, formula 5.6 yields a more conservative estimate of reliability than formula 5.5. Formula 5.6, which was derived from formula 5.5 by making p_i the same for all items, is simpler from a computational standpoint, because the k products $p_i(1 - p_i)$ do not have to be calculated.

To illustrate the application of formula 5.6, let us assume that a test containing 70 items has a mean of 50 and a variance of 100. then

$$r_{11} = \frac{70}{69}\left[1 - \frac{50(70-50)}{70(100)}\right] = .87.$$

Therefore, the estimated reliability of this test, by K-R formula 21 (formula 5.6), is .87.

Coefficient Alpha Formulas 5.5 and 5.6 are specific cases of the more general coefficient alpha (Cronbach, 1951). *Coefficient alpha* may be defined as

$$\alpha = \frac{k}{k-1}\left[1 - \sum_{i=1}^{k}\frac{s_i^2}{s_t^2}\right], \qquad (5.7)$$

where s_i^2 the variance of scores on item i and s_t^2 is the variance of total test scores. Although the Kuder-Richardson formulas are applicable only when test items are scored 0 ("wrong") or 1 ("right"), coefficient alpha is a general formula for estimating the reliability of a test consisting of items on which two or more scoring weights are assigned to answers. Internal consistency procedures (split-half, Kuder-Richardson, coefficient alpha) overestimate the reliability of speeded tests. Consequently these procedures need to be modified somewhat to provide good reliability estimates when a test is speeded. One recommendation is to administer two halves of the test at different but equal times. Then the scores on the two separately timed halves are correlated, and the resulting correlation coefficient is corrected by the Spearman-Brown or Flanagan formulas. Test-retest and parallel-forms procedures may also be used to estimate the reliability of a speeded test.

Interscorer Reliability of Essay and Oral Tests

In scoring an objective test, different scorers will—barring clerical errors—compute the same score for a given test paper. But scoring essay and oral tests, in addition to certain other evaluative judgments (personality ratings and scoring projective tests, for example), is a fairly subjective process. Consequently, it is wise to have such judgments made independently by at least two people. The correlation between scores assigned by two scorers provides an index of interscorer agreement referred to as an interscorer or *interrater reliability coefficient.* When there are more than two scorers, an intraclass correlation or a coefficient of concordance is an appropriate reliability index. The computation of these indexes will not be described here, but the procedures may be found in many statistics or psychometrics books (e.g., Winer, 1971).

Oral tests are not renowned for their high reliabilities, but special forms for rating performance can improve their objectivity and, hence, reliability (see Deitz, 1961; Green, 1975; Guerra, Abramson & Newmark, 1964). Although oral examinations typically have lower reliabilities than comparable written tests, careful attention to the design of oral questions, the construction of model answers to questions before the test is administered, and the use of multiple raters or scorers have resulted in interscorer reliability coefficients in the .60s and .70s in certain college, graduate-level, and professional school courses (Carter, 1962; Levine & McGuire, 1970; Hitchman, 1966). Other suggestions for improving the reliabilities of oral examinations include requiring examinees to delay answering until they have thought about the question (Meredith, 1978) and tape recording answers for later playback and reevaluation by scorers.

Standard Error of Measurement

Reliability cannot be computed directly from formula 5.2 because the variance of true scores is unknown. Given an estimate of test reliability, however, true score variance can be computed from formula 5.2, or, of greater interest, error variance can be computed from formula 5.3. Solving formula 5.3 for s_{err} gives

$$s_{err} = s_{obs}\sqrt{1 - r_{11}}. \quad (5.8)$$

This statistic, known as the *standard error of measurement,* is an estimate of the standard deviation of the normal distribution of test scores that an examinee would obtain if she or he took the test many different times.[4] The mean of this hypothetical distribution is the examinee's true score on the test.

The standard error of measurement is a useful statistic because it enables an examiner to estimate limits within which the true scores of a certain percentage of examinees having a given observed score can be expected to fall, assuming that errors of measurement are normally distributed. According to theory, 68 percent of a group of examinees having the same observed score will have true scores falling within ± 1 standard error of measurement of that observed score. Likewise, 95 percent of a group of examinees having a given observed score will have true scores falling within approximately $\pm$ 2 standard errors of measurement of that observed score.

As an example, assume that the standard deviation of observed scores on a test is 10 and the reliability coefficient is .90; then $s_{err} = 10\sqrt{1 - .90} =$ 3.16. So if a person's observed score is 50, it can be concluded with 68 percent confidence that this person is one of a group of examinees with an observed score of 50 whose true scores lie between 46.84 and 53.16. Furthermore, it can be concluded with approximately 95 percent confidence that the person is one of a group of examinees with an observed score of 50 whose true scores lie between 43.68 and 56.32.

An examinee's score on certain tests is expressed not as a single number but rather as a score band, or *percentile band,* having a width of 1 standard error of measurement (or the percentile rank equivalents of s_{err}) on either side of the examinee's observed test score. This practice is merely an acknowledgment of the fact that a score on a test is not a fixed, unvarying measure of a characteristic but only an approximation. The standard error of measurement is an index of the average error in that approximation.

When a person's scores on several tests are plotted in the form of a profile, it is useful to draw a band having a width of 1 or 2 standard errors of measurement around the score points. Then small differences between the scores of the same person on two different tests or the scores of two persons on the same test are less likely to be viewed as significant. In general, the difference between the scores of two persons on the same test should not be interpreted as significant unless it is at least twice the standard error of measurement of the test. On the other hand, the difference between the scores of the same person on two different tests should be greater than twice the standard error of measurement of either test before it can be viewed as significant. This is true because the standard error of the difference between the scores on two tests is larger than the standard error of measurement of either test alone.[5]

As formula 5.8 shows, the standard error of measurement increases as reliability decreases. When $r_{11} = 1.00$, there is no error at all in estimating an examinee's true score from his or her observed score. When $r_{11} = .00$, the error of measurement is a maximum and equal to the standard deviation of observed scores. Of course, a test with a reliability coefficient close to .00 is useless because the correctness of any decisions made on the basis of the scores will be no better than chance.

How high must the reliability coefficient be in order for a test to be useful?

The answer to this question depends on what one plans to do with the test scores. If a test is used to determine whether the mean scores of two groups of people are significantly different, then a reliability coefficient as low as .65 may be satisfactory. If the test is used to compare one examinee with another, a coefficient of at least .85 is necessary.

Table 5–1 lists representative reliability coefficients for different types of tests. In general, tests of cognitive abilities are more reliable than affective measures. As Table 5–1 shows, however, even cognitive tests may have low reliabilities in certain contexts, and the reliabilities of personality tests and other affective measures are sometimes quite high.

Score Variability and Reliability

Reliability was defined in formula 5.2 as the ratio of true score variance to observed score variance. Now if the variance of observed scores is increased by a certain amount, say s_c^2, but error variance remains the same, the variance of true scores will also be increased by that same amount. Formula 5.2 then becomes $r_{11} = (s_{\text{tru}}^2 + s_c^2)/(s_{\text{obs}}^2 + s_c^2)$. Since adding the same constant to both the numerator and the denominator of a fraction increases the size of that fraction, r_{11} becomes larger whenever observed variance increases and error variance is unchanged.

In constructing or modifying a test, there are several ways of increasing its observed score variance without appreciably affecting its error variance. A test composed of items of moderate difficulty has a greater variance than tests composed of very difficult or very easy items. Furthermore, the length of a test affects its variance and, consequently, its reliability. The general Spearman-Brown formula is an expression of the effect on reliability of lengthening a test by adding more items of the same type. This formula, a generalization of formula 5.4, is

TABLE 5–1 Reliability Coefficients Obtained with Various Psychological Assessment Instruments

Type of Instrument	*Reliabilities*		
	Low	*Median*	*High*
Achievement test batteries	.66	.92	.98
Scholastic ability tests	.56	.90	.97
Aptitude test batteries	.26	.88	.96
Objective personality tests	.46	.85	.97
Interest inventories	.42	.84	.93
Attitude scales	.47	.79	.98

Source: G. C. Helmstadter, *Principles of Psychological Measurement,* © 1964, p. 85. Adapted by permission of Prentice-Hall, Inc. Englewood Cliffs, New Jersey.

$$r_{mm} = \frac{mr_{11}}{1 + (m - 1)r_{11}}, \qquad (5.9)$$

where m is the factor by which the test is to be lengthened, r_{11} the reliability of the original test, and r_{mm} the estimated reliability of the lengthened test. For example if a test with reliability .80 is made three times as long, the expected reliability of the lengthened test is $r_{mm} = 3(.80)/[1 + 2(.80)] = .92$. By solving formula 5.9 for m, one can also compute how many times longer a test of reliability r_{11} must be made in order to attain a desired level of reliability (r_{mm}).

In addition to being dependent on test difficulty and length, the variance and reliability of a test are affected by the heterogeneity of the group of people who take the test. The greater the range of individual differences among a group of people on a certain characteristic, the larger will be the variance of their scores on a measure of that characteristic. Consequently, the reliability coefficient of a test or other measure will be higher in a more heterogeneous group, which has a larger test score variance, than in a more homogeneous group with a smaller test score variance. The fact that the reliability of a test varies with the nature of the group tested is reflected in the practice of reporting separate reliability coefficients for different age, grade, sex, and occupational groups.

Reliability of Criterion-Referenced Tests

The traditional concept of reliability pertains to norm-referenced tests, which are designed primarily to differentiate among individuals who possess various amounts of cognitive or affective characteristics. The greater the range of individual differences in test scores, the higher is the test's reliability. The aim of the test constructor in the case of most criterion-referenced tests, however, is to place the examinees into one of two groups: those who have attained the criterion (mastery) level of the skill and those who have not. In this situation, traditional correlational procedures used in determining test-retest, parallel forms, and internal consistency coefficients are inappropriate. Instead, the following reliability formula, adapted from a procedure outlined by Lindeman and Merenda (1979), is suggested:

$$c = \frac{nb - sf}{nb + v(n + b + v)}, \qquad (5.10)$$

where n = the number of examinees who reach the criterion level on neither administration of the test, b = the number of examinees who reach the criterion level on both administrations of the test, f = the number of examinees who reach the criterion level on only the first administration of the test, s = the number of examinees who reach the criterion level on only the second administration of the test, and v = the smaller value of f or s.

To illustrate the computation of this c coefficient, assume that on a criterion-referenced test administered to 100 students, $n = 5$, $b = 75$, $s = 5$, $f = 15$, and therefore $v = 5$. Then the c coefficient for this test is

$$c = \frac{5(75) - 5(15)}{5(75) + 5(5 + 75 + 5)} = \frac{300}{800} = .375,$$

indicating a rather low reliability.

Generalizability Theory

Also representing a deviation from the classical approach to reliability, but remaining in the norm-referenced tradition of an emphasis on individual differences, is generalizability theory. *Generalizability theory* considers a test score to be one sample from a universe of possible scores, and the reliability of that score is the precision with which it estimates a more generalized universe value of the score (the "true score"). Generalizability theory uses the statistical procedures of analysis of variance to determine the generalizability or dependability of test scores as a function of changes in the person(s) taking the test, different samples of items comprising the test, the situations or conditions under which the test is administered, and the methods or people involved in scoring the test. A *generalizability coefficient,* similar to a traditional reliability coefficient, is then computed as the ratio of the expected variance of scores in that universe to the expected variance of scores in the sample. Finally, a "universe value" of the score, similar to the "true score" of classical reliability theory, can be estimated (Cronbach et al., 1972).

Wiggins (1973) has discussed some of the advantages of generalizability theory and its role as a bridge between the traditional concepts of reliability and validity. Still, although much of the language of generalizability theory has been absorbed into the field of testing, the concepts and methods have not replaced classical test theory and its emphasis on the distinction between test reliability and validity.

VALIDITY

Traditionally the *validity* of a test has been defined as the extent to which the test measures what it was designed to measure. A shortcoming of this definition is its implication that a test has only one validity, which is presumably established by a single study to determine whether the test measures what it was designed to measure. In actuality, however, a test has many different validities, depending on the specific purposes of the test and varying with the method of assessing validity. Among the methods for studying the validity of a test are analyzing its content, relating scores on the test to scores on a criterion of interest, and investigating the particular psychological characteristics or constructs measured by the test. All of these procedures for assessing validity are useful to the extent that they improve one's understanding of what a test measures. If we understand what the test measures, then the scores will provide better information for making decisions concerning the examinees. Furthermore, in considering the validity of a test, one needs to ask how much the particular test adds to the prediction and understanding of criteria that are already being predicted. This is the notion of incremental validity, to which we shall return later.

Unlike reliability, which is influenced only by unsystematic errors of measurement, the validity of a test is affected by both unsystematic and systematic (constant) errors. A test may therefore be reliable without being valid, but it cannot be valid without being reliable. Another way of making the same point is to state that reliability is a necessary condition but not a sufficient condition for validity. Technically, the (criterion-related) validity of a test, as indicated by the correlation between the test and an external criterion measure, can never be greater than the square root of the parallel forms reliability coefficient of the test.

Content Validity

Whether a test "looks good" for a particular purpose *(face validity)* is certainly an important consideration in marketing the test. The concept of *content validity,* however, refers to more than just face validity. The question of a test's content validity is concerned with whether the stimulus materials or situations comprising the test call for a range of responses that represent the entire domain or universe of skills, understandings, or other behaviors that the test is supposed to measure. That universe of behaviors must be carefully specified. Then, if the test is well designed, examinees' responses to the items on the test will be representative of what their responses would be to the universe of situations sampled by the test.

An analysis of content validity occurs most often in connection with achievement tests, in which case there is usually no external criterion measure. The content validity of tests of aptitude, interest, and personality should, however, also be of concern. The content validity of an achievement test is assessed by determining the degree to which the test represents the objectives of instruction; the content of the test is compared with an outline or table of specifications concerning the subject matter presumably covered by the test (see Chapter 2). This procedure involves the judgments of subject-matter experts; if they agree that the test looks and acts like a measure of the skill or knowledge it is supposed to assess, then the test is said to possess content validity. Such judgments may involve not only the content of the test items but also an analysis of the processes examinees are likely to go through in arriving at answers. Obviously, the determination of a test's content validity need not necessarily wait until the test has been constructed. Expert judgments concerning what items to include on a test are made from the beginning of the test construction procedure. By defining the universe of content of the test and the sample of content to be included, the test constructors are engaging in the process of content validation from the start.

Criterion-Related Validity

Basically, all tests are validated by relating scores on the tests to performance on criterion measures—standards or variables against which test performance can be evaluated. In the case of content validity, the criterion is the judgment of subject-matter experts. Traditionally, however, the term *criterion-related validity* has been restricted to validation procedures in which the test scores of a group of examinees are compared with ratings, classifications, or other test scores assigned to the examinees. Examples of criteria against which tests are validated are school marks, supervisors' ratings, and number of sales made. Whenever the criterion measure, whatever it may be, is available at the time of testing, then the *concurrent validity* of the test is being determined. When the criterion does not become available until some time after the test is administered, the *predictive validity* of the test is of interest.

Concurrent Validity Concurrent validation procedures are employed whenever a test is administered to people in various categories, such as diagnostic groups or socioeconomic levels, for the purpose of determining whether the average test scores of people in different categories differ significantly. If the average score varies substantially from category to category, then the test might be used as another, perhaps more efficient, means of classifying people into these categories. For example, scores on the Minnesota Multiphasic Personality Inventory (MMPI) are useful in the classification of mental disorders because it has been determined that people diagnosed by psychiatrists as having a specific mental disorder tend to make characteristic scores on certain groups of items *(scales)* on the MMPI.

Predictive Validity *Predictive validity* is concerned with the accuracy, as expressed by the correlation between the test (predictor) and a measure of performance (criterion), with which test scores predict criterion scores. Predictive validity is of concern primarily with respect to aptitude or intelligence tests, since pretest scores on these kinds of tests are often correlated with ratings, marks, achievement test scores, and other criteria of success.

The correlation between a predictor variable and a criterion variable, computed by a procedure such as that described in Chapter 1 for the Pearson r, varies with the specific criterion but is seldom greater than about .60. Because the proportion of variance in the criterion that can be accounted for by the predictor equals the square of the correlation between predictor and criterion, typically not more than 36 percent of the variation in criterion scores can be predicted from scores on a test or other prediction instrument. This leaves 64 percent of the criterion variance unaccounted for or unpredicted. Considering that the predictive validity of most tests is less than .60, it is understandable why claims for the ability of psychological tests to predict behavior should be made cautiously.

Standard Error of Estimate The section on linear regression in Chapter 1 describes the procedure for determining a regression equation (prediction equation) to predict examinees' criterion scores from their scores on a test or another predictor variable. However, a predicted score obtained by substituting a person's test score in such an equation is only an estimate of the criterion score that will actually be obtained. If an individual's predicted criterion score is viewed as the mean of a normal distribution of criterion scores obtained by people with the same score on the predictor test, then the standard deviation of this distribution is an index of the average error in the predictions. This standard deviation, known as the *standard error of estimate* (s_{est}), is approximately equal to

$$s_{est} = s\sqrt{1 - r^2}, \tag{5.11}$$

where s is the standard deviation of the criterion scores and r the product-moment correlation between the predictor (test) and the criterion.

To illustrate the computation and meaning of s_{est}, suppose that the standard deviation of a criterion measure is 15 and the correlation between test and criterion is .50. Then $s_{est} = 15\sqrt{1 - (.50)^2} \approx 13$. Therefore, if an examinee's predicted criterion score is 50, the chances are 68 out of 100 that he or she will obtain a criterion score between 37 and 63 ($Y_{pred} \pm 1s_{est}$) and approximately 95 out of 100 of obtaining a criterion score between 24 and 76 ($Y_{pred} \pm 2s_{est}$). More precisely, it means that the chances are 68 out of 100 that the examinee is one of a group of persons with the same test score whose obtained criterion scores fall between 37 and 63. Similarly, the chances are approximately 95 our of 100 that the examinee is one of a group of people making the same test score whose obtained criterion scores fall between 24 and 76. This example shows that when the correlation between test and criterion is low, a person's obtained criterion score may be quite different from his or her predicted score. For this reason, one must be very careful in interpreting predicted scores when the correlation between test and criterion is modest. The smaller the correlation coefficient is, the larger is the standard error of estimate and the less accurate is the prediction.

Factors Affecting Criterion-Related Validity The criterion-related validity of a test can be affected by a number of factors: group differences, test length, and criterion contamination. The incremental validity of a test should also be considered in deciding whether to use the test for selection or placement purposes.

Group Differences The criterion-related validity of a test varies with the characteristics of the group of people on whom the test is validated. Differences between groups of examinees on variables such as sex, age, and personality traits—referred to in this context as *moderator variables*—may affect the correlation between the test and the criterion. The magnitude of a validity coefficient, like that of a reliability coefficient, is also influenced by the degree of heterogeneity of the validation group on the test variable. The validity coefficient tends to be smaller in a more homogeneous group—that is, a group having a narrower range of test scores. Actually, since the size of a correlation coefficient is a function of two variables, a narrowing of the range of either the predictor or the criterion variable will tend to lower the validity coefficient.

Because the magnitude of a validity coefficient varies with the nature of the group tested, a newly constructed test that is found to be a valid predictor of a particular criterion variable in one group of examinees should be cross-validated. *Cross-validation* involves administering the test to a second sample of people to determine whether the test retains its validity across different samples. Due to the operation of chance factors, the magnitude of a validity coefficient usually shrinks somewhat on cross-validation. Consequently, the correlation between test and criterion obtained on cross-validation is considered in most instances to be a better index of the test's predictive validity than the original test-criterion correlation. Cross-validation, one way of determining a test's validity generalization, may also involve a different (parallel) sample of test items. In either case—different samples of examinees, different samples of test items, or both—there is typically some shrinkage of the validity coefficient on cross-validation. Formulas for "correcting" for such shrinkage have been proposed, but they entail certain assumptions that cannot always be met.

Test Length Validity, like reliability, varies directly with test length because, in general, the longer a test is, the greater is its variance. Formulas that correct for the effects of range restriction and curtailed test length on test validity have been proposed, but they are appropriate only under certain special conditions.

Criterion Contamination The validity of a test is limited not only by the reliabilities of the test and the criterion but also by the validity of the criterion itself as a measure of the particular variable of interest. Sometimes the criterion is made less valid, or "contaminated," by the particular method in which criterion scores are determined. For example, college teachers have been known to inspect students' scores on the Scholastic Aptitude Test (SAT) before deciding what course grades to assign. Because SAT scores are also used by college admissions officers to select students who are predicted to make satisfactory grades, this method of assigning grades can contaminate the criterion, resulting in an inaccurate validity coefficient. Grades, and other performance criteria, generally should be determined without reference to scores on aptitude tests or other predictor variables.

Incremental Validity Judgments concerning the usefulness of a test for predicting a specific criterion require knowing not only the test-criterion correlation but also how expensive and time-consuming it is to administer the test compared to other, perhaps simpler, procedures. If the test is to be used in combination with other methods, then some measure of its *incremental validity*—how much the test adds to the validity of already existing prediction methods—is helpful (Secrest, 1963).

Construct Validity

The most general type of validity, in that it uses evidence from studies of the content validity and the criterion-related validity of a test, is *construct validity*. The construct validity of a test is determined by defining as clearly as possible the characteristic or trait (construct) to be measured and then relating the test scores to measures of behavior in situations where that construct is thought to be an important variable. As an example, evidence for the construct validity of a test of anxiety can be obtained by determining whether persons who score high on a test of anxiety, in contrast to those who score low on the test, behave in a manner similar to the way highly anxious people theoretically are supposed to behave in certain stressful situations. The construct validity of a test is not established by one successful prediction; it consists of the slow, laborious process of gathering evidence from many experiments and observations on how the test is functioning. Among the sources of evidence for the construct validity of a test are the following:

1. Experts' judgments that the content of the test pertains to the construct of interest.
2. An analysis of the internal consistency of the test.
3. Studies of the relationships, in both experimentally contrived and naturally occurring groups, of test scores to other variables on which the groups differ.
4. Correlations of the test with other tests and variables with which the test is expected to have a certain relationship and factor analyses of these intercorrelations.
5. Questioning examinees or raters in detail about their responses to a test or rating scale in order to reveal the specific mental processes that occurred in deciding to make those responses.

A test that possesses construct validity should not only correlate highly with other tests or measures of the same characteristic *(convergent validation)*, but it should also have low correlations with measures of different characteristics *(discriminant validation)*. Four types of correlations are of interest in determining the convergent and discriminant validity of a test. These are the correlations between measures of:

1. The same trait by the same method.
2. Different traits by the same method.
3. The same trait by different methods.
4. Different traits by different methods.

Using this *multitrait-multimethod approach* (Campbell & Fiske, 1959), evidence for the construct validity of a test is obtained when one finds that the correlations between the same trait measured by the same and different methods are higher than the correlations between different traits measured by the same or different methods. The actual results, however, are often the reverse of what is expected; the correlations between different traits measured by the same method are sometimes higher than the correlations between the same trait measured by different methods. When this occurs, the method by which the characteristic or trait is measured has a more consistent effect on examinee's responses than the hypothesized trait itself. Such a result casts doubt on the importance of that characteristic as a stable determinant of behavior.

USING TESTS IN PERSONNEL DECISIONS

Of all types of validity, criterion-related validity has received the greatest attention in psychological and educational measurement. One reason is that concurrent and predictive validity can be cast in a statistical framework for both theoretical and practical purposes. In this section the application of information on criterion-related validity to the making of personnel decisions will be discussed.

If a person's score on a criterion measure can, within a certain margin of error, be predicted from a score on a test, then the test can be used to select people who will perform satisfactorily on the criterion or to classify and place people according to their predicted criterion scores. The use of tests in personnel selection and classification is an important topic in the field of personnel psychology, but only a few basic principles will be introduced here. Readers desiring more information on the topic are encouraged to refer to Landy (1985) and McCormick & Ilgen (1980).

Historical Background

Selecting and placing people to perform various organizational duties has been occurring since antiquity but often in a rather haphazard and unscientific manner. The ancient Chinese were reportedly the first to use systematic procedures to evaluate people for public service jobs (DuBois, 1970). The principal method of assessing the skills and abilities of government employees in ancient China consisted of a series of oral examinations administered to employees every three years. Other nations have used a variety of techniques for personnel selection and appraisal, many based on casual observation and intuition. For example, great importance was sometimes given to head shape, eye movements, and overall body appearance. Cultural and familial origins were also significant in determining who was appointed to a position, hired for a specific job, or accepted for a certain educational program.

Screening

Personnel selection traditionally has been concerned with identifying, from a pool of applicants, those who are most able to perform certain designated tasks.

In this approach, psychological tests have been used, together with nontest information (background, physical characteristics, recommendations, and so on), to help select applicants who can—in some cases after appropriate training—perform satisfactorily.

A personnel selection procedure may be fairly simple or quite complex, depending on the task for which people are being selected and the organization. The most straightforward approach is the sink-or-swim strategy in which every applicant is selected or admitted but only those who perform effectively are retained. This is an ideal selection strategy in some ways, but it is also expensive—to both the organization and the applicant. Consequently, almost all organizations use some kind of *screening* procedure by which applicants who are clearly unsuited for the task (job, program, and so on) are immediately rejected. If a psychological test is used as the screening instrument, applicants who obtain a certain score *(cutoff score)* or higher on the test are accepted, whereas those whose scores fall below the cutoff score are rejected. There is a certain impersonality to this procedure, and it may occasionally seem unkind from an applicant's viewpoint. However, both product-making and service-providing organizations must run efficiently in order to accomplish their goals, and they run most efficiently when the members of the organization perform effectively.

Classification and Placement

Initial screening usually is followed by the *classification* and assignment of those who have been selected into one of several job or educational categories. Classification decisions may involve grouping people on the basis of their scores on more than one psychological test, such as classifying military inductees into occupational specialties on the basis of their scores on the Armed Services Vocational Aptitude Battery (ASVAB). Screening and classification frequently are followed by the *placement* of those who have been selected at a particular level of a specific job or program. An example is placing pupils in remedial, regular, and accelerated classes according to their scores on an educational achievement test.

The process of personnel selection usually consists of a sequence of stages entailing a series of "yes-no" decisions based on information provided by application forms, references, interviews, psychological tests, and other predictors of occupational or educational success. The purpose of collecting this information is identical to that of any other application of psychology: to make accurate predictions of future behavior from data on past and present behavior. The more reliable and valid the information is, the greater is the likelihood of making correct predictions of on-the-job or in-the-program behavior and hence the sounder will be the selection decisions. The reliability and validity of psychological assessment instruments and procedures for making selection decisions cannot, of course, be discovered by merely inspecting the assessment materials; they must be determined empirically, which is one of the primary tasks of the personnel psychologist.

An Expectancy Table

When tests are used for purposes of selection, it is not essential to determine the test-criterion correlation and the regression equation linking predicted criterion scores to test scores. Correlational methods are applicable to the construction of theoretical expectancy tables, but an empirical *expectancy table* can be constructed without computing a correlation coefficient or any other statistic except frequencies and percentages. Table 5–2 was constructed from a joint frequency distribution of scores on the Scholastic Aptitude Test–Verbal (SAT–V) and the freshman year grade-point averages of 250 college students. The SAT–V score intervals are listed on the left side of the table, and the grade-point averages across the top. The nonitalicized frequencies in the cells of the table are the numbers of students having SAT–V scores in a given 50-point range whose grade-point averages fall within a given range of .5 point. For example, the grade-point averages of ten people whose SAT–V scores are in the interval

TABLE 5–2 Empirical Expectancy Table

SAT Verbal score	*Freshman year grade-point average* F	D		C		B		A
	0.00–0.49	*0.50–0.99*	*1.00–1.49*	*1.50–1.99*	*2.00–2.49*	*2.50–2.99*	*3.00–3.49*	*3.50–3.99*
750–799						1 *(100)*		2 *(67)*
700–749					2 *(100)*		5 *(82)*	4 *(36)*
650–699				1 *(100)*	8 *(94)*	3 *(50)*	4 *(33)*	2 *(11)*
600–649	False Positives			4 *(100)*	10 *(85)*	7 *(48)*	5 *(22)*	1 *(4)*
550–599			6 *(100)*	12 *(88)*	16 *(63)*	13 *(31)*	2 *(4)*	
500–549		4 *(100)*	7 *(94)*	25 *(83)*	21 *(45)*	5 *(12)*	3 *(5)*	
450–499		5 *(100)*	10 *(87)*	14 *(61)*	7 *(24)*	2 *(5)*		
400–449	1 *(100)*	6 *(96)*	8 *(72)*	5 *(40)*	4 *(20)*	1 *(4)*		
350–399	2 *(100)*	5 *(85)*	4 *(46)*	2 *(15)*				
300–349	1 *(100)*				False Negatives			

600–649 fall between 2.00 and 2.49, whereas fourteen people with SAT–V scores between 450 and 499 have grade-point averages between 1.50 and 1.99.

The italic numbers in parentheses in Table 5–2 are the percentages of people with SAT–V scores in a given interval whose grades fall within that interval or higher. Thus, 85 percent of the people whose SAT–V scores fall in the interval 600–649 made grade-point averages of 2.00 or higher, and 61 percent of those having SAT–V scores between 450 and 499 made grade-point averages of 1.50 or higher.

To illustrate how this type of information might be used in counseling and selection, assume that Cathy, a high school graduate from a group similar to the one on which Table 5–2 was constructed, makes a score of 460 on the SAT–V. Her chances of obtaining a freshman year grade-point average of 1.50 or higher (C or higher) are approximately 61 out of 100, but her chances of obtaining a grade-point average of 2.50 or higher are only 5 out of 100. It would be predicted that she will pass, but her chances of being a superior student during her freshman year are not very great.

Factors Affecting the Accuracy of Prediction

It has been demonstrated that the accuracy with which an examinee's criterion score can be predicted depends on the size of the correlation between predictor and criterion. The higher the validity coefficient, the more accurate is the prediction. The predictive accuracy of a test is also affected by a number of other factors, including false positive and false negative errors, the selection ratio, and the base rate.

False Positives and Negatives If the cutoff score on a test is set very low, there will be many incorrect acceptances, or *false positives.* These are applicants who were selected but do not succeed on the job or in the program. On the other hand, if the cutoff score is set very high, there will be many incorrect rejections or *false negatives.* These are applicants who were not selected but would have succeeded had they been selected. Since the purpose of selection is to obtain as many "hits" as possible—to reject potential failures and select potential successes—the determination of a cutoff score must be made carefully.

To illustrate these concepts, refer again to Table 5–2. Suppose that it is planned to set the cutoff score on the SAT–V at 450 and that 1.50 is considered to be a minimum passing grade-point average (GPA). Then 4 + 5 + 6 + 7 + 10 = 32 of the students whose scores are given in Table 5–2 will be classified as false positives; they scored at least 450 on the SAT–V but had a GPA of less than 1.50. On the other hand, 5 + 2 + 4 + 1 = 12 students are false negatives; they scored below 450 on the SAT–V but had GPAs of 1.50 or greater. Observe that if the cutoff SAT–V score were raised, the result would be a decrease in the number of false positives but an increase in the number of false negatives. The opposite effect—an increase in false positives and a decrease in false negatives—would occur if the cutoff score on the SAT–V were lowered.

Selection Ratio The establishment of a cutoff score on a test or test composite depends not only on the validity of the test(s) but also on the *selection ratio*—the proportion of applicants to be selected. The lower the selection ratio is, the higher is the cutoff score; the higher the selection ratio is, the lower is the cutoff score. Since the cutoff score affects the number of false positive and false negative errors, one might argue that the selection ratio should be determined by the relative seriousness with which these two types of selection errors are viewed. Is it more serious to accept an applicant who will fail (false positive) or to reject an applicant who would have succeeded (false negative)? Such errors should be taken into consideration, but at least as important in determining the selection ratio is the size of the applicant pool. For example, when the labor market is tight, the number of applicants is small. In this case the selection ratio will need to be high, and consequently the cutoff score on the test low, in order to select the desired number of people for a position. On the other hand, in a free, or open, labor market, the selection ratio will be low and the cutoff score on the test high.

Figure 5–1 illustrates the relationship of the selection ratio and the validity of a selection test to the percentage of applicants selected who will be successful on a particular job or in a certain program. The specific job or program is one in which 50 percent of the applicants who have already been selected are successful. This figure, which has been adapted from a portion of the Taylor-Russell tables (Taylor & Russell, 1939), shows that the percentage of successful applicants increases as the test's validity coefficient increases and the selection ratio decreases. Charts such as this one permit an employment manager or

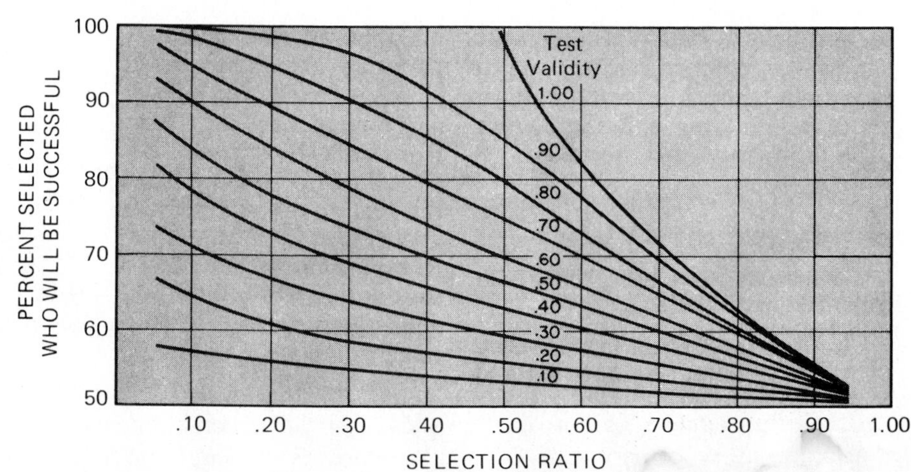

FIGURE 5–1 **Relationship of Test Validity and Selection Ratio to Percentage of Selected Applicants Who Will Be Successful.**
(After Ernest J. McCormick/Daniel R. Ilgen, *Industrial Psychology,* 7th edition, © 1980, p. 133. Reprinted by permission of Prentice-Hall, Inc., Englewood Cliffs, New Jersey.)

academic admissions director to determine what percentage of selected employees or students can be expected to be successful when a certain proportion of applicants are selected by using a test having a certain validity coefficient.

Base Rate Another important factor affecting the accuracy of a test in identifying people who will behave in a certain way is the base rate. The *base rate* is the proportion of people in the population of interest who would act in a certain manner (for example, be successful on the job) if given the opportunity. A test designed to predict a particular type of behavior is most effective when the base rate is 50 percent and least effective when it is either very high or very low. For example, a test designed to select people to perform a highly complex task, which relatively few people can perform adequately, would not be as effective as a test designed to select people for a job that half the applicant population can do satisfactorily. Another illustration is a clinical test designed to identify potential suicides. Because the incidence of suicide in the general population is quite low, such a test would not be very effective. On the other hand, a test designed to identify neurotics should do better, because the percentage of neurotics in the general population is substantial.

Multiple Cutoff and Multiple Regression

Deciding where to set the cutoff score on a selection or placement test can be a complicated statistical and judgmental process. In addition to the factors discussed, the cutoff score and the usefulness of a test in general are affected by what other instruments and information are available to supplement the test scores.

Multiple Cutoff Frequently a group of scores or measures are combined in making selection and classification decisions. One procedure, referred to as *successive hurdles* or *multiple cutoff,* is to set separate cutoff scores on each of several measures. Then an applicant must score at the cutoff point or beyond on each of the separate tests or measures in order to be selected. The multiple cutoff approach is most appropriate in prediction situations where a high score on one variable cannot compensate for a low score on another variable. For example, the ability to hear well is essential to effective performance as a sonar operator. Regardless of intellectual ability, an examinee with poor hearing will not do well in that occupation.

Multiple Regression A more mathematical approach to combining the scores of a large sample of people on several measures is to determine a *multiple regression equation* in which different statistically assigned weights are applied to scores on different tests. Once these weights are determined, a single predicted criterion score for each applicant can be computed from the regression equation by multiplying the applicant's score by the appropriate regression weights. For example, a multiple regression equation employed for admissions purposes at one college was Y_{pred} = .002SAT–V + .001SAT–M + .030HSR − 2.00, where Y_{pred} designates freshman year grade-point average, SAT–V and SAT–M are the Verbal and Mathematical scores on the Scholastic Aptitude Test, respectively, and HSR is a *T* score measure of rank in high school graduating class. Assume that an applicant's scores on the two parts of the SAT are 600 and 500 and that his or her rank in high school class is 70. Then, according to the equation, the person's predicted grade-point average is .002(600) + .001(500) + .030(70) − 2.00 = 1.8, a low C.

In the multiple regression approach, a high score on one predictor variable can compensate for a low score on another variable. Therefore, this approach to prediction should not be used in situations where a minimum score on any of the predictors is essential for effective performance on the criterion. When the multiple regression approach is chosen, a *multiple correlation coefficient* (*R*)—an index of the relationship of a weighted combination of the predictor variables to the criterion measure—should be computed. *R* ranges from .00 to +1.00 and is interpreted in a manner similar to the product-moment *r* to indicate the accuracy with which the criterion can be predicted from a specific combination of predictor variables.

SUMMARY

The reliability of a test is its relative freedom from errors of measurement. In classical test score theory, reliability is defined as the ratio of a test's true score variance to its observed score variance. Because true score variance cannot be computed directly, reliability must be estimated by one of several procedures that take into account various sources of measurement error. The three traditional methods for estimating the reliability of a test or other assessment device are test-retest, parallel forms, and internal consistency. Of these methods, parallel forms, which considers errors due to different times of administration as well as errors due to different samples of test items, is the most satisfactory. However, parallel forms of a test are expensive and time-consuming to construct. Internal consistency approaches, which are less appropriate for speeded tests, include split-half, Kuder-Richardson, and coefficient alpha.

A test's standard error of measurement, which varies inversely with the magnitude of the reliability coefficient, is used to compute confidence intervals for true scores on a test. The larger a test's standard error of measurement is, the wider is the range of scores that can be said, with a specified degree of confidence, to contain an examinee's true score.

Reliability varies directly with the number of items on the test and the heterogeneity of the group taking the test. Reliability also varies with the difficulty level of the items comprising the test, being maximal with items of intermediate difficulty.

Procedures for determining the consistency among different scorers or raters (interscorer or interrater reliability) and the reliability of criterion-referenced tests were discussed briefly in this chapter. Brief attention was also given to generalizability theory, which conceptualizes a test score as a sample from a population and therefore an estimate of a true score or universe value.

Reliability is a necessary but not a sufficient condition for validity—the extent to which a test measures what it was designed to measure. Information on the validity of a test may be obtained in various ways: by analyzing the test's content *(content validity)*, by correlating test scores with scores on a criterion measure obtained at the same time as the test scores *(concurrent validity)*, by correlating test scores with scores on a criterion measured at a later time *(predictive validity)*, and by a systematic study of the adequacy of the test as a measure of a specified psychological construct *(construct validity)*. Achievement tests are usually content validated, whereas predictive validity is of greater interest on aptitude tests. Concurrent and construct validity are important on personality tests.

The error made in predicting a person's criterion score from his or her test score is estimated by the standard error of estimate, which varies inversely with the size of the criterion-related validity coefficient. Both the criterion-related validity coefficient and the standard error of estimate are affected by a number of factors, including group differences, test length, and criterion contamination. Validity coefficients can also be affected by chance factors, and therefore tests used for predictive purposes should be cross-validated. It is also important to consider how much test scores contribute to the process of making good decisions about people (incremental validity).

Information on the construct validity of a test as a measure of a particular psychological construct (characteristic or trait) can be obtained in a variety of ways. Especially helpful is an analysis of correlations between the test and other measures of the same construct obtained by the same or different methods, as well as measures of different constructs obtained by the same or different methods (multitrait-multimethod matrix).

Personnel selection consists of the screening, classification, and placement of applicants for a job or training program. "Yes-no" decisions pertaining to hiring or acceptance are often facilitated and made more accurate by using a screening test. Applicants who are selected for a job or training program may then be classified, or assigned to particular jobs, on the basis of their scores on other tests. Tests can also help in placing employees at certain levels within job categories.

The effectiveness of screening, classification, and placement decisions made with the assistance of tests depends on the validity of the tests, the relative importance of false positive and false negative errors, the selection ratio, and the base rate. Selection strategies such as multiple cutoff and multiple regression, are applied when there are multiple predictors. Expectancy tables, which give the percentage of applicants falling in a given predictor score range who make at or above a specified criterion score, are helpful in selecting employees or students.

EXERCISES

1. Calculate the Kuder-Richardson reliability, using both formulas 5.5 and 5.6, of the data given in Exercise 3 of Chapter 4. Compare the results with the split-half coefficient obtained from applying formulas 1.6 and 5.4 in succession to total scores on the odd-numbered and the even-numbered items.
2. Plot a graph illustrating how test reliability varies as a function of test length, using initial reliabilities (r_{11}) of .50, .60, .70, .80, and .90 and lengthening factors (m) of 2, 3, 4, 5, and 6 (use formula 5.9). The horizontal axis of your graph should be m, the vertical axis r_{mm}, and one curve corresponding to each value of r_{11} should be drawn. What conclusions concerning the effects of r_{11} and m on r_{mm} can be drawn from an inspection of your graph?
3. Construct an empirical expectancy table from the paired X, Y scores in Table 1–6. Use X as the predictor (row) variable and Y as the criterion (column) variable. Use an interval width of 7 in setting up the score intervals for both the X and Y variables (see Table 5–2).
4. What is the estimated split-half reliability of a test if the correlation between total scores on the odd-numbered items and total scores on the even-numbered items is .70?
5. Use formula 5.6 to estimate the internal consistency reliability of a fifty-item multiple-choice test having a mean of 38.75 and a variance of 50.30.
6. A criterion-referenced test is administered twice to the same group of 100 examinees. The criterion level is reached by 70 examinees on both administrations, 10 examinees on the first administration only, 15 examinees on the second administration only, and 5 examinees on neither administration of the test. What is the reliability coefficient of the test?
7. A test consisting of forty items has a reliability coefficient of .80. Approximately how many more items of the same general type must be added to the test to increase its reliability to .90?
8. The reliability coefficient of a certain ten-item attitude scale is .75. A psychologist wants to increase its reliability to at least .85. Can he or she accomplish this by adding five more items to the scale?
9. If the standard deviation of a mechanical reasoning test is 12.0 and the reliability coefficient is .84, what is the standard error of measurement of the test? If Johnny obtains a score of 36 on the test, the chances are 95 out of 100 that he is one of a group of examinees whose true scores on the test fall between what limits?
10. What is the standard error made in estimating grade-point averages from scores on an aptitude test if the standard deviation of the criterion is .50 and the correlation between test and criterion is .60? Interpret this result.
11. Examine several standardized test manuals for information on the relia-

bilities of various tests. Prepare a table showing how reliability varies with type of test, age/grade of the standardization group, and other relevant variables. Also record any information on test validity reported in the test manual, and make a note of the kinds of norms that are given.

NOTES

1. Flanagan (1937) proposed an alternative to the Spearman-Brown split-half reliability formula (formula 5.4). Flanagan's formula, which does not require making the assumption of equal variances in the two halves of the test or necessitate computing the correlation between scores on the two halves, is

$$r_{11} = 2\left(1 - \frac{s_o^2 + s_e^2}{s_t^2}\right),$$

where s_o^2 is the variance of the scores on one half, s_e^2 the variance of scores on the other half, and s_t^2 the variance of scores on the whole test.,
2. An estimate of the reliability of a test can also be computed as

$$r_{11} = \frac{k\bar{r}_{ij}}{1 + (k - 1)\bar{r}_{ij}},$$

where k is the number of items and $\bar{r}_{ij}$ the average of all correlations among items. For a test of fifty items, $\bar{r}_{ij}$ is the mean of 1,225 correlation coefficients.
3. The variances (s^2) in these two formulas should be computed by using n, the total number of scores, rather than $n - 1$ in the denominator of the variance formula (square of formula 1.4).
4. Even when the reliability and standard deviation of a test are unknown, a good estimate of the standard error of measurement is $s_{err} = .432\sqrt{k}$, where k is the number of items on the test (Lord, 1959).
5. The proof of this point is based on the fact that the reliability of the difference between the scores on two tests is significantly less than the reliability of either test by itself. For example, if the reliability of test 1 is $r_{11} = .90$, the reliability of test 2 is $r_{22} = .80$, and the correlation between the two tests is $r_{12} = .70$, then the reliability of the difference between the scores on tests 1 and 2 is

$$r_{dd} = \frac{r_{11} + r_{22} - 2r_{12}}{2(1 - r_{12})} = \frac{.90 + .80 - 2(.70)}{2(1 - .70)} = .50.$$

SUGGESTED READINGS

Aiken, L. R. (1985). Three coefficients for analyzing the reliability and validity of ratings. *Educational and Psychological Measurement, 45,* 131–142.

Allen, M. J., & Yen, W. M. (1979). *Introduction to measurement theory.* Monterey, CA: Brooks/Cole.

American Educational Research Association, American Psychological Association, & National Council on Measurement in Education (1985). *Standards for educational and psychological testing* (pp. 9–24). Washington, DC: American Psychological Association.

American Psychological Association. Division of Industrial-Organizational Psychology. (1980). *Principles for the validation and use of personnel selection procedures.* 2d ed. Berkeley, CA: Author.

Dudek, F. J. (1979). The continuing misinterpretation of the standard error of measurement. *Psychological Bulletin, 86,* 335–337.

Ghiselli, E. E., Campbell, J. P., & Zedeck, S. (1981). *Measurement theory for the behavioral sciences.* San Francisco: Freeman.

Green, B. F. (1981). A primer of testing. *American Psychologist, 36,* 1001–1011.

Livingstone, S. A. (1985). Reliability of test results. In T. Husen & T. N. Postlethwaite (eds.), *International encyclopedia of education* (vol. 7, pp. 4268–4275). New York: Wiley.

Zeller, R. A. (1985). Validity. In T. Husen & T. N. Postlethwaite (eds.), *International encyclopedia of education* (vol. 9, pp. 5413–5422). New York: Wiley.

Part II

Assessment of Abilities

Chapter 6

Standardized Achievement Tests

Chapters 1 through 5 have been concerned primarily with the methodology of psychological and educational testing, including statistics, test construction, test administration, and the evaluation of test scores. Now we shall consider some of the more applied aspects of testing by surveying specific types of tests and what they measure. Achievement testing, known as attainment testing in the United Kingdom, is considered in this chapter; other cognitive instruments—tests of general intelligence and special abilities—are discussed in Chapters 7 through 9.

ACHIEVEMENT TESTING IN PERSPECTIVE

Tests of *achievement*, defined as the level of knowledge, skill, or accomplishment in an area of endeavor, are the most popular of all types of tests. If one considers all the classroom tests constructed by teachers and the standardized tests sold to schools and other organizations, the number of achievement tests administered easily surpasses other types of psychological and educational measures. As an indication of the number of standardized achievement tests alone that are available, *The Ninth Mental Measurements Yearbook* (Mitchell, 1985) lists 68 achievement batteries, 134 language tests, 97 reading tests, 46 mathematics tests, 26 science tests, and dozens of tests in other subject-matter areas.

All tests of ability—general intelligence, special abilities, and achievement—are actually measures of what individuals have achieved. The items on tests of intelligence and special abilities, like those on achievement tests, require that examinees demonstrate some accomplishment. Scores on achievement tests may also be used for many of the same purposes as scores on intelligence tests, the former often being better predictors of school marks than the latter. This does not mean, however, that tests of achievement in a specific subject can completely replace tests of intelligence and special abilities. The accomplishments or achievements measured by general intelligence tests are usually broader and produced by less formal, and probably less recent, learning experiences than those measured by standardized tests of achievement. Furthermore, because achievement tests usually assess knowledge of something that has been explicitly taught, scores on these tests are more influenced by coaching than are scores on general intelligence tests.

A distinction between achievement tests and tests of intelligence and special abilities can also be made in terms of their focus. Achievement tests focus more on the present—what a person knows or can do now—whereas tests of intelligence and special abilities focus on the future—what a person should be able to do with further education or training.

Historical Overview

Until the latter half of the nineteenth century, oral examinations were almost the only method used to evaluate pupil achievement. In the middle of the nineteenth century, the Boston educator Horace Mann argued persuasively that written examinations, administered and scored under uniform conditions, were more objective measures of achievement than oral examinations. But oral examinations continued to be the customary way of assessing school achievement, and only gradually were they superseded by written tests.

The first objective test of achievement, a handwriting scale, was constructed by the Englishman George Fisher in 1864. The next important step was taken over a quarter century later, when the American J. M. Rice (1897) constructed objective tests of spelling for his classic survey of the spelling abilities of schoolchildren. The results of administering a fifty-word spelling test to 33,000 children led Rice to conclude that as much was learned in 15 as in 40 minutes of daily instruction in spelling. In later studies, Rice assessed the language skills of 8,000 children and the arithmetic achievement of 6,000 children. Rice's work is generally viewed as the forerunner of standardized achievement testing, which was subsequently developed by E. L. Thorndike and other educational psychologists.

A number of standardized achievement tests appeared during the early years of the twentieth century. For example, Stone's arithmetic test became available in 1908 and Thorndike's Scale of Handwriting for Children in 1909. By the end of the 1920s numerous standardized achievement tests had been published, including batteries of tests such as the Stanford Achievement Test (1923) for elementary school pupils and the Iowa High School Content Examination for high school students. The new multiple-choice format, together with the invention of automated scoring machines, led to a rapid increase in the use of standardized tests for assessing school achievement.[1]

One finding that led educators to question the reliability of essay examinations was an empirical demonstration that the level of agreement among teachers in the marks that they assigned to essay examination papers was not very high (Starch & Elliott, 1912). Although the question of the relative merits of essay and objective tests was never fully settled, it became apparent that objective tests can measure not only memory for facts but also many of the more complex effects of education that were formerly presumed to be tapped only by essay examinations. A noteworthy trend in recent years has been toward tests that measure higher-order objectives, such as application, analysis, and evaluation. Another trend has been away from standardized achievement tests that attempt to meet broad educational objectives and toward tests designed specifically for particular textbooks and teaching programs. Finally, in response to the criticism that objective tests foster poor habits of writing and self-expression, greater emphasis is now being placed on standardized essay tests of written expression.

Uses of Achievement Tests

Achievement tests serve numerous functions, the basic one being to determine how much people know about certain topics or how well they can perform certain skills. The test results inform students, as well as their teachers and parents, about students' scholastic accomplishments and deficiencies. Such tests can also motivate students to learn, provide teachers and school administrators with information to plan or modify the curriculum for a student or group of students, and serve as a means of evaluating the instructional program and staff. Scores on educational tests obviously are not the sole means of evaluating the effectiveness of instruction, but they do provide one measure of the quality of education and thereby may contribute to its improvement.

Achievement tests admittedly do not assess all the objectives or goals proposed by educational philosophers. For example, they do not directly measure such affective variables as joy and confidence in thinking, interest in educational subject matter, pleasure in using skills, the enjoyment of reading, learning to learn and to cope with change, or the development of interpersonal and social competence. What these tests can measure, however, and much more accurately than teachers' ratings or other subjective judgments, is the extent to which examinees have achieved the cognitive objectives of instruction (Levine, 1976).

Teacher-made and Standardized Tests The functions of achievement tests referred to in the preceding paragraph apply to both classroom tests prepared by teachers and standardized tests constructed by professionals in educational measurement, but teacher-made tests differ from standardized tests in certain important respects. A teacher-made test is more specific to a particular teacher, classroom, and unit of study and is easier to keep up to date. Consequently a teacher-made test is more likely to reflect the current educational objectives of a given school or teacher. Standardized tests, on the other hand, are built around a core of general educational objectives common to many different schools. The objectives represent the combined judgments of subject-matter experts, who cooperate with test construction specialists in developing the test. Standardized achievement tests also focus more on understanding and thinking processes than on knowledge of specifics. Clearly, teacher-made and standardized tests complement rather than replace each other. Both methods of measuring achievement should be employed depending on the objectives of the particular class or school. It is possible that a given standardized test does not measure the educational goals of a particular school system, in which case other standardized or teacher-made tests should be considered.

In addition to being more carefully constructed and having broader content coverage than teacher-made tests, standardized achievement tests have norms and higher reliability coefficients. For these reasons, standardized achievement tests are especially helpful in comparing individual pupils for the purpose of class placement and in evaluating different curricula by assessing the relative achievements of different groups or schools. The diagnostic function of a test, whereby a person's abilities and disabilities in a certain subject or area are determined, may be served by both teacher-made and standardized tests, although standardized tests have proved somewhat more valuable for that purpose. Decisions pertaining to the individualization of instruction, placement at particular instructional levels, and remedial instruction usually are made on the basis of scores on standardized rather than teacher-made tests.

Accountability and Performance Contracting Test scores have been used not only to evaluate students but also to evaluate teachers and schools. *Accountability,* or holding teachers accountable for their degree of success in teaching students, has been a controversial topic in education. As a result of increasing public concern over the failure of schools to do an adequate job of educating certain students, particular attention has been given in recent years to accountability for teaching effectiveness. Efforts have been made in many school systems to specify the competencies that students should attain in order to complete a given grade or course of study or to graduate from high school. Instruction and evaluation of instruction are then based on the achievement of these competencies.

An emphasis on accountability and competency-based instruction leads directly to *performance contracting:* making the paychecks of teachers commensurate with their degree of success in teaching students. If tests are to be employed as a means of determining the extent to which a teacher has fulfilled a contract to teach the course material to students, the same tests may be administered at the beginning and end of the course. Consequently, the higher are the gains from pretest to posttest in the achievements of students, the greater is the teacher's pay.

When combined with other measures of performance, achievement tests can and should contribute to decisions concerning accountability. However, they have definite limitations when used for this purpose. One serious statistical limitation is that pretest to posttest gain scores usually have substantially lower reliability than either the pretest or posttest scores themselves (see note 5, Chapter 5).

Summative and Formative Evaluation Traditionally an achievement test is administered at the end of a unit or course of study to determine whether students have attained the objectives of instruction. Technically this procedure is known as *summative evaluation:* a test score is viewed as an end product, or a summing up, of large units of educational experience. In contrast to summative evaluation, a need for *formative evaluation* is a consequence of the belief that the processes of instruction and evaluation should be integrated. The purpose of formative evaluation is "to help both the learner and the teacher focus upon the particular learning necessary for movement toward mastery" (Bloom, Hastings & Madaus, 1971, p. 61). When evaluation is formative, testing and other methods of assessing educational progress occur continuously while instruction is proceeding. A direct result of the notion of formative evaluation is the development of instructional units including testing as an integral part rather than as a termination. In this way a learner's performance is constantly evaluated during the learning process and can serve to direct him or her toward review and further learning.

Norm-Referenced and Criterion-Referenced Measurement Not only has educational measurement traditionally been summative, but it has also been norm referenced rather than criterion referenced. As described in Chapter 5, a person's score on a norm-referenced test is interpreted by comparing it with the distribution of scores obtained from some norm (standardization) group. A person's score on a criterion-referenced test is interpreted by comparing it with an established standard or criterion of effective performance. In terms of content, norm-referenced tests are typically broader and contain more complex tasks than criterion-referenced tests. Consequently, the range of individual differences in scores on a norm-referenced test tends to be greater than that on a criterion-referenced test.

Despite differences in purpose and design, a particular achievement test can function as both a norm-referenced and a criterion-referenced instrument. How much material a student has learned (criterion-referenced function) and how his or her performance compares with that of other students (norm-referenced function) can sometimes be determined from the same test (Carver, 1974).

Examples of commercially available criterion-referenced tests are CTB/McGraw-Hill's Prescriptive Reading Inventory, PRI Reading Systems, Diagnostic Mathematics Inventory, DMI Mathematical Systems, and Riverside Publishing Company's Reading Yardsticks. Although there are more criterion-referenced tests of reading and mathematics than other subject areas, tests of this type in language arts, social studies, and science are also available. Riverside Publishing

Company prepares customized criterion-referenced tests, referred to as Multiscore, in reading, language arts, mathematics, science, social studies, and life skills according to user selections from nearly 1,800 instructional objectives and a nationally standardized bank of more than 5,500 test items. A similar service is provided by Science Research Associates' mastery: Custom Program.

Custom-built criterion-referenced tests possess an advantage in being tailored to the objectives of a particular school system, but they also have a number of disadvantages. In addition to the problem of deciding on an acceptable passing score or mastery level on each test, the need for a large number of subtests in order to measure many different educational objectives makes each subtest relatively short and hence its reliability fairly low. Furthermore, the problems of how the reliabilities and validities of these subtests and the test as a whole should be determined have not been completely resolved.

The National Assessment of Educational Progress A criterion-referenced approach has guided the National Assessment of Educational Progress (NAEP), a continuing nationwide survey of the knowledge, skills, understandings, and attitudes of young Americans. Currently financed by the National Institute of Education and housed at Educational Testing Service in Princeton, New Jersey, the NAEP project has involved the periodic assessment of 20,000 to 32,000 people from each of four age groups (9, 13, 17, and 25–35 years) in ten subject areas: art, career and occupational development, citizenship, literature, mathematics, music, reading, science, social studies, and writing. Two or three subjects have been assessed in a given year since 1969 and reassessed on a three- to six-year cycle.

A stratified random-sampling procedure has been employed by NAEP in selecting examinees: a certain number of persons of each sex, socioeducational status, and race are chosen at random from four geographical regions and four types of communities. Although a large number of questions concerning each topic are asked, the procedure of sampling both examinees and items makes only one relatively short testing period (50 minutes) necessary for each person. Adults are assessed individually, and younger people are assessed on both an individual and a group basis. Since the results are expressed in terms of the percentages of examinees at each level who possess certain skills and knowledge, the names of examinees do not appear on the test papers.

National Assessment was planned as a continuing program to provide the American public, especially legislators and educators, with information on the status and growth of educational accomplishments in the United States and the extent to which the nation's educational goals are being met. These surveys were not designed, as some have feared, to evaluate the achievements of specific schools or school districts or as a means of federal control over public school curricula. The findings, however, have been analyzed by geographical area, size and type of community, sex, parental education, and race. Of particular interest are analyses of the effects of federal support and specific types of programs on educational attainment.

Types of Standardized Achievement Tests

There are four general types of achievement tests: survey test batteries, survey tests in specific subjects, diagnostic tests, and prognostic tests. The characteristics of each type of test are discussed below, and specific instruments are described later in the chapter. Since the market for highly specialized tests in a particular subject area is rather limited, standardized achievement tests are more likely to cover broad content areas and to deal with matters of general knowledge. And because the curriculum becomes more specialized in the upper grade levels, administration of standardized achievement tests is less common after junior high school.

Survey Test Batteries The most comprehensive way of assessing achievement is to administer a *survey test battery,* a group of subject-matter tests designed for particular grade levels. The major purpose of administering a battery of tests is to determine an individual's general standing in a group rather than his or her specific strengths and weaknesses. Consequently, each test in a survey battery contains a rather limited sample of the content and skills in a given subject. Because the various tests in a battery are standardized on the same sample of examinees and the scores are expressed on the same numerical scale, a person's performance in different subject areas can be compared directly.

Single Survey Tests Although they provide a broader survey of pupil achievement than single tests, test batteries have a number of drawbacks. Despite the longer total administration time, the tests comprising a battery are shorter than single survey tests and consequently have lower reliabilities. Of course, not all the tests contained in a battery need to be administered to a given group of students; the examiner may select just those tests that are required. In addition to the individual subject tests in a survey battery, the examiner has a choice of a number of single subject-matter tests. These survey tests are usually longer and more detailed than the comparable tests of a battery and thus may permit a more thorough evaluation of achievement in a specific area. Single survey tests, however, typically yield only one overall score and make no attempt to determine the specific causes of high or low performance in the subject. Because of greater cross-school uniformity in reading and mathematics instruction than in other subjects, standardized tests in these two areas tend to be more valid than, for example, science and social studies tests.

Diagnostic Tests Certain tests have the diagnostic function of identifying specific difficulties in learning a subject. To construct a *diagnostic test* in a basic skill such as reading, arithmetic, or spelling, performance on the subject as a whole must be analyzed into subskills and then groups of items devised to measure performance on these subskills. Unlike survey tests, which usually provide only one score, a diagnostic test yields a score on each of the several subskills comprising the test. Since differences between scores on the various parts of the test are interpreted in making diagnoses, the number of items for measuring a particular subskill must be sufficient (ten or more) to make the differences between part scores reliable. Unfortunately, the number of items comprising part scores are often small and scores on the parts are correlated, resulting in difference scores of low reliability (see note 5, Chapter 5).

Most diagnostic tests are in the area of reading, but diagnostic tests in mathematics and spelling have been constructed. A diagnostic test contains a greater variety of items and usually takes longer to administer than a survey test in the same subject. It may also involve special apparatus such as a tachistoscope and an eye-movement camera.

The administration of a survey test battery is a logical first step in a testing program because it gives an overall picture of an examinee's standing in various subjects. If a second assessment of a person's achievement in a particular area is needed, a single test in that specific subject can then be administered. Finally, if it is desirable to make a detailed analysis of an individual's disability in reading or mathematics and to determine the causes of the disability, a diagnostic test should be administered.

Prognostic Tests Prognostic tests, which are designed to predict achievement in specific school subjects, contain a wider variety of items than a typical achievement test in the same subject. They are similar to aptitude tests in their function as predictors of later achievement. For example, the purpose of a *reading-readiness test* administered to a kindergartner or first-grader is to predict whether the child is ready to profit from instruction in reading. At a higher grade level, prognostic tests in mathematics (algebra, geometry) and foreign languages are designed to predict facility in learning those subjects.

Selecting a Standardized Achievement Test

Before describing specific instruments, some of the problems encountered in selecting a standardized achievement test need to be considered. As in constructing a classroom achievement test, selecting a standardized achievement test is basically a matter of finding a test of appropriate difficulty with a content that matches the instructional objectives of the particular organization, class, school, or school system. This means that the level of knowledge or ability of the examinees and the content and objectives of the curriculum must be determined before deciding what test(s) to use. Furthermore, the reasons for testing and the way the scores are to be used should be considered; there is little purpose in administering a test merely because it "looks good" and then permanently filing the unused results.

Purposes and Practical Considerations The manual accompanying a test frequently details its possible uses—pupil evaluation, placement, diagnosis of learning difficulties, determination of readiness to learn, curriculum evaluation—and refers to supporting evidence. Consequently, before a test is selected, the specific ways in which the scores are to be used should be clarified and test manuals consulted to determine what tests are appropriate for these purposes. In addition to reading the manual, prospective purchasers should examine a copy of the test and even take it themselves to determine whether it is suitable for its intended use. Most testing companies publish specimen sets of their tests, consisting of a test booklet, an answer sheet, a manual, a scoring key, and other materials; test catalogs are also available on request. These materials are valuable in helping to make decisions on what tests to administer.

Another consideration in choosing a test is the degree of cooperation that can be expected from the school staff in administering the test and interpreting the findings. Also of importance are practical matters such as cost and time for administration, scoring, and analyzing the results. The machine-scoring services provided by commercial testing firms greatly facilitate the scoring and analysis processes and are usually fairly reasonable in cost.

Reliability, Validity, and Norms Frequently overlooked in selecting a test, but often crucial, are its statistical characteristics. Most achievement tests have reliability coefficients in the .80s or .90s, but the meaning of these high coefficients depends on the procedures by which the coefficients were obtained. A parallel-forms coefficient is preferable to a test-retest or internal-consistency coefficient because the last two are more likely to be spuriously high. As for validity, content validity is of greatest importance in achievement testing.[2] Therefore, determination of the validity of an achievement test consists of comparing the content of the test with the objectives of the particular instructional program. An adequately prepared test manual will report the system of classifying content and behavioral objectives that was employed in constructing the test, and purchasers must decide whether these objectives correspond to their own.

Another statistical characteristic to be examined in selecting any test is the adequacy and appropriateness of the norms. Most well-constructed achievement tests have been standardized on representative, nationwide samples, sometimes stratified according to age, sex, geographical region, socioeconomic status, and other relevant variables. If a test purchaser plans to report scores in terms of these norms, he or she should make certain that the characteristics of the norm group are similar to those of the students to be examined. For purposes of placement and other comparisons within a given school or school system, local norms may be even more meaningful than national norms.

Test users also need to be very clear on the point that in plotting a student's academic growth by means of normed scores on a standardized achievement test administered at successive grade levels, it is assumed that the different grade-level groups on which the test was standardized are equivalent. If there is any reason to believe that there were significant differences among the norm groups in variables other than those that are growth related, then a student's grade-norm scores, percentile-rank scores, or standard scores on a test cannot be validly compared across grade levels.

Another caveat of test purchasing is to exercise caution in selecting a test on the basis of its name. Experienced test users are well aware of the "jingle fallacy" of assuming that tests having the same name measure the same thing, and the "jangle fallacy" of assuming that tests having different names measure different things. Before deciding what achievement tests to purchase, novices and experienced testers alike can profit from consulting *The Mental Measurements Yearbooks* and test reviews in professional journals.

ACHIEVEMENT TEST BATTERIES

Achievement test batteries, sometimes referred to as *general educational development* (GED) *tests,*[3] represent attempts to measure broad cognitive abilities and skills that do not depend on specific subject-matter courses. These multilevel batteries of tests assess basic skills in reading, mathematics, language, and, at the appropriate age levels, study skills, social studies, and science.

The testing programs of many schools are based on an achievement test battery administered during the fall or spring to students in grades 3 through 12 for the purpose of measuring general educational growth. Such tests have many different uses: grouping (placement), identification of individuals for more detailed study, curriculum evaluation, and curriculum planning. The test results are of interest to teachers, parents, and curriculum advisers and, of course, to the students themselves. A limitation of the battery approach is that some of the tests may not match the particular objectives of the school or school system. Furthermore, not all tests in a given battery are of equal reliability or content validity.

Battery Norms

The various subtests comprising a particular level of an achievement test battery are standardized simultaneously on the same group of examinees. Consequently, the resulting unified set of norms permits direct evaluation of an examinee's relative achievement in several subject areas. Since different grade levels of a test battery are standardized on comparable groups of examinees, the scholastic growth of students may be charted by comparing their scores on the tests over a period of several years; however, this should not be done if there is any question about the equivalence or comparability of the different grade-level samples of students on whom the test battery was standardized. Furthermore, the norms against which students' scores are compared should have been obtained from administering the test(s) to the standardization group during the same time of year as the students whose scores are being evaluated were tested.

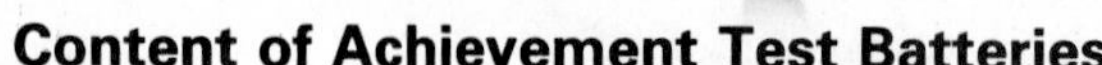

Content of Achievement Test Batteries

Elementary School Level Because of the greater uniformity of instructional content in elementary school, achievement test batteries are administered more frequently at this level. A typical elementary school battery consists of subtests for measuring reading vocabulary, reading comprehension, language usage, spelling, arithmetic fundamentals, and arithmetic comprehension. Subtests to measure study skills, social studies, and science may also be included, but the emphasis at the elementary level is on the measurement of achievement in basic verbal and quantitative skills. Figure 6–1, for example, gives a breakdown of the scores of one student on the Stanford Achievement Test. It illustrates the

Stanford ACHIEVEMENT TEST
WITH OTIS-LENNON SCHOOL ABILITY TEST

SKILLS ANALYSIS FOR CHARLES A BALLARD

TEACHER MS WELLENS
SCHOOL LAKESIDE ELEMENTARY — GRADE 4 — TEST DATE 10/12/82 — COPY 1
SYSTEM NEWTOWN PUBLIC SCHOOLS — STANFORD NORMS GR 4.1 — LEVEL PRIM 3 — FORM E
OLSAT NORMS GR 4 FALL — LEVEL ELEM — FORM S

(B)

TESTS NUMBER OF ITEMS (A)	RAW SCORE	SCALE SCORE	NAT'L PR-S	GRADE EQUIV	ACHIEVMNT ABILITY COMPARISN
WORD STUDY SKILLS 54	35	142	50- 5	4.1	LOW
READING COMPREHENSION 60	49	143	50- 5	4.0	LOW
VOCABULARY 38	29	148	52- 5	4.3	LOW
LISTENING COMPREHENSION 40	31	139	44- 5	3.9	LOW
SPELLING 36	18	143	40- 5	3.8	LOW
LANGUAGE 46	37	148	60- 6	4.6	MIDDLE
CONCEPTS OF NUMBER 34	14	137	32- 4	3.5	LOW
MATH COMPUTATION 42	20	145	50- 5	3.9	MIDDLE
MATH APPLICATIONS 38	19	145	50- 5	4.0	LOW
SOCIAL SCIENCE 44	36	161	82- 7	5.5	MIDDLE
SCIENCE 44	19	130	34- 4	3.3	LOW
USING INFORMATION 40	27	160	77- 7	5.0	MIDDLE
TOTAL READING 114	84	143	50- 5	4.0	LOW
TOTAL LISTENING 78	60	144	48- 5	4.1	LOW
TOTAL LANGUAGE 82	55	146	52- 5	4.2	LOW
TOTAL MATHEMATICS 114	53	143	44- 5	3.8	LOW
BASIC BATTERY TOTAL 388	252	NA[2]	50- 5	4.0	NA[2]
COMPLETE BATTERY TOTAL 476	308	NA[2]	50- 5	4.0	NA[2]
OTIS-LENNON (C)	AGE	PR-S	84-7	RS = 51	SAI = 116
SCHOOL ABILITY TEST	GRADE	PR-S	82-7		

NATIONAL PERCENTILE BANDS: 1 5 10 20 30 40 50 60 70 80 90 95 99 (D)

AGE 9 YRS. 1 MO.

READING SKILLS GROUP—DEVELOPMENTAL (E)

CONTENT CLUSTERS (F)	RAW SCORE/NUMBER OF ITEMS	BELOW AVERAGE	AVERAGE	ABOVE AVERAGE
WORD STUDY SKILLS	35/54		✓	
Structural Analysis	7/18	✓		
Phonetic Analysis—Consonants	16/18			✓
Phonetic Analysis—Vowels	12/18		✓	
READING COMPREHENSION	49/60		✓	
Textual Reading	15/20		✓	
Functional Reading	17/20			✓
Recreational Reading	17/20		✓	
Literal Comprehension	28/30			✓
Inferential Comprehension	21/30		✓	
VOCABULARY	29/38		✓	
LISTENING COMPREHENSION	31/40		✓	
Retention	17/20		✓	
Organization	14/20		✓	
SPELLING	18/36		✓	
Sight Words	6/ 8		✓	
Phonetic Principles	4/16	✓		
Structural Principles	8/12		✓	
LANGUAGE	37/46		✓	
Conventions	22/26		✓	
Language Sensitivity	7/10		✓	
Reference Skills	8/10			✓
CONCEPTS OF NUMBER	14/34		✓	
Whole Numbers and Place Value	8/18		✓	
Fractions	1/ 5	✓		
Operations and Properties	5/11		✓	

WRITING TEST RESULTS:

CONTENT CLUSTERS	RAW SCORE/NUMBER OF ITEMS	BELOW AVERAGE	AVERAGE	ABOVE AVERAGE
MATHEMATICS COMPUTATION	20/42		✓	
Addition with Whole Numbers	9/12		✓	
Subtraction with Whole Numbers	8/ 9			✓
Multiplication with Whole Numbers	2/12	✓		
Division with Whole Numbers	1/ 9	✓		
MATHEMATICS APPLICATIONS	19/38		✓	
Problem Solving	9/18		✓	
Geometry/Measurement	5/14	✓		
Graphs and Charts	5/6			✓
SOCIAL SCIENCE	36/44			✓
Geography	6/ 6			✓
History and Anthropology	6/ 9		✓	
Sociology	5/ 6			✓
Political Science	3/ 4			✓
Economics	8/10			✓
Inquiry Skills	8/ 9			✓
SCIENCE	19/44		✓	
Physical Science	4/11	✓		
Biological Science	9/18		✓	
Inquiry Skills	6/15		✓	
USING INFORMATION	27/40			✓

See back for aids for interpretation.

DATA SERVICES DIVISION — THE PSYCHOLOGICAL CORPORATION, HARCOURT BRACE JOVANOVICH, PUBLISHERS

Sample Skills Analysis on Stanford Achievement Test. **FIGURE 6–1**

variety of linguistic and mathematical skills measured by an achievement test battery at the elementary school level. Test batteries for measuring the achievements of preschool children are also available. An example is the Tests of Basic Experiences (TOBE 2), published by CTB/McGraw-Hill. The pictorial response items on the TOBE 2 are divided into four areas: mathematics, language, science, and social studies.

Secondary School Level Because of greater variability in the academic programs of different high school students, achievement test batteries are less useful at this level. The test batteries continue to emphasize basic skills in reading language, and arithmetic, but tests in social studies, science, and study skills are also common. At both the elementary and secondary school levels achievement tests emphasize general educational development and are not tied to specific courses in particular schools. The sample items in Table 6–1 illustrate the kinds of questions appearing at successive levels in five of the tests on one achievement battery, the Comprehensive Tests of Basic Skills. Also of interest at the high school level are batteries of tests such as the American College Tests (ACT), which are administered annually for college admissions purposes. The ACT is actually an achievement test battery, but it is somewhat like an aptitude test in that its broad range of content is less related to specific school experiences than that of most achievement tests.

Selected Achievement Test Batteries

There is insufficient space here to describe all of the noteworthy achievemen test batteries, but the following five are good examples in terms of conten coverage, statistical characteristics, and currentness (see Appendix A for pub lishers' addresses).

***Comprehensive Tests of Basic Skills* (CTBS–U & V)** (by the staff of CTB McGraw-Hill, 1981–1982) This third edition of the CTBS was, like its predeces sors, designed to measure the basic skills in the broad areas of reading, spelling language, mathematics, science, social studies, and reference skills. The Reading tests are composed of vocabulary and reading comprehension items; the Spelling tests measure the application of rules for consonants, vowels, and structura forms; the Language tests contain items for assessing skills in the mechanics and expression of language; the Mathematics tests measure computational skill and applications of concepts and conventions; the Science tests measure knowledge of science content (botany, zoology, physics, chemistry, ecology), as well as understanding of scientific language, concepts, and methods; the Social Studies tests contain items pertaining to concepts in geography, economics, history political science, and sociology. The ten levels (A–K) of the CTBS battery of tests cover the entire range of school grades, from kindergarten through high school, and the two forms (U and V) permit retesting. An item-response mode (see Chapter 4) was employed in the development and standardization of the

Examples of Items on the Comprehensive Tests of Basic Skills TABLE 6–1

Test 1. READING Vocabulary (Selecting the word that means the same or about the same as the underlined word)

Level 1 (Grades 2.5–4)

mend the tire

○ patch
○ clean
○ change
○ fill

Level 2 (Grades 4–6)

approved his behavior

F conscience
G rights
H decision
J actions

Level 3 (Grades 6–8)

adequate supplies

F adjusted
G actual
H sufficient
J extra

Level 4 (Grades 8–12)

complete solitude

F pacification
G seclusion
H confusion
J classification

Test 3. LANGUAGE Mechanics (Identifying mistakes in capitalization)

Level 1 (Grades 2.5–4)

In America we ○ | celebrate a holiday ○ | on July 4. ○ | None ○

Level 2 (Grades 4–6)

F This selection comes | G from "the silent world,"
H a book about exciting | J deep-sea diving adventures. | K None

Level 3 (Grades 6–8)

A The villain was | B finally apprehended at | C Dulles international airport
D near Washington. | E None

Level 4 (Grades 8–12)

F When football magazine | G featured him on its cover, | H his fame became
J truly nationwide. | K None

Test 5. LANGUAGE Spelling (Identifying misspelled words)

Level 1 (Grades 2.5–4)

○ *full*
○ *cake*
○ *football*
○ *rabit*
○ *None*

Level 2 (Grades 4–6)

A jerney
B event
C contain
D spoon
E none

TABLE 6–1 *Continued*

Test 5. LANGUAGE Spelling (Identifying misspelled words)

Level 3 (Grades 6–8)

F recommend
G allowance
H literature
J profit
K None

Level 4 (Grades 8–12)

F constantly
G interpret
H benefit
J explenation
K None

Test 7. ARITHMETIC Concepts

Level 1 (Grades 2.5–4)

What goes in the box?
5+4= 10−□

0	1	9	10
○	○	○	○

Level 2 (Grades 4–6)

What should be next in this series:
57, 64, 71, 78, ____?

F 79
G 81
H 85
J 88

Level 3 (Grades 6–8)

In 5963.427 the digit in the hundredths place is

A 2
B 5
C 6
D 7

Level 4 (Grades 8–12)

If $R<S$ and $S<T$, then

F $R=T$
G $R>T$
H $R<T$
J $R+S=T$

Test 9. STUDY SKILLS (Using reference materials)

Level 1 (Grades 2.5–4)

Which one of these words would be *first* in abc order?

pair	paint	polish	point
○	○	○	○

Level 2 (Grades 4–6)

Which reference book would you use to find information on: A history of shipbuilding?

A almanac
B dictionary
C encyclopedia
D atlas

Level 3 (Grades 6–8)

The library catalog subject card for Amusements would be found in the tray labeled

F A—ALK
G ALL—ANH
H ANI—ANS
J ARO—BAH

Level 4 (Grades 8–12)

In preparing a report about Carl Sandburg, which would be a primary source of information?

F a collection of his writings
G a review of a collection of his poems
H a talk with an old friend of his
J a biography by a well-known writer

Source: Comprehensive Tests of Basic Skills, Form R. Reproduced by permission of the publisher, CTB/McGraw-Hill.

CTBS–U & V. In addition, special efforts were made to construct a bias-free instrument and to collect norms on representative samples of the entire U.S. school population. Testing time ranges from 1 hour, 8 minutes for level A to 4 hours, 50 minutes for levels F through K.

Iowa Tests of Basic Skills (ITBS) (by A. N. Hieronymus, H. D. Hoover, & E. F. Lindquist, Riverside Publishing Co., 1986). The ITBS, designed to assess the basic skills considered essential in any type of school work, was published originally in 1935 as the Iowa Every-Pupil Tests of Basic Skills. The newest edition, Forms G and H, consists of tests at ten levels, grouped as a Primary Battery and a Multilevel Edition. The early Primary Battery (Levels 5–6), for grades K.1–1.9, consists only of a Basic Battery. Included in the Basic Battery are five tests (Listening, Word Analysis, Vocabulary, Language, Mathematics) at Level 5 and these five tests plus a Reading test at Level 6. Levels 7–8 of the Primary Battery and Levels 9–14 of the Multilevel Edition are available in Basic and Complete Batteries. Seven tests are included in the Basic Battery and thirteen tests in the Complete Battery at Levels 7–8 (grades 1.7–3.5). The Basic Battery of the Multilevel Edition (Levels 9–14, grades 3–9) consists of six tests, the Complete Battery of eleven tests. Total working time is 134–135 minutes for the Complete Battery and 227–246 minutes for the Complete Battery, depending on the level. Forms G and H of the ITBS were standardized in 1985 concurrently with the Tests of Achievement and Proficiency (TAP) and the Cognitive Abilities Test (CogAT).

Metropolitan Achievement Tests, 6th ed. (MAT6) (by G. A. Prescott et al., The Psychological Corporation, 1985) This achievement test battery consists of two components: a Survey battery covering a range of objectives from kindergarten through grade 12 and a Diagnostics package consisting of three batteries. The Diagnostics package provides norm-referenced scores that are compatible with those of the Survey battery. There are two forms (L and M) of the Survey battery at each of the six levels from Primary 1 (grades 1.5–2.9) to Advanced 2 (grades 10.0–12.9); there is one form for the Preprimer (grades K.0–K.9) and Primer (grades K.5–1.9) levels. Testing time for the complete battery ranges from 1 hour, 38 minutes at the Preprimer level to 4 hours, 14 minutes at the Elementary level. Scores on Total Reading, Total Language, and Total Basic Battery are obtained at all levels, in addition to a Total Complete Battery score at Primary 1 to Advanced 2 levels. The specific tests and subtest scores vary with the level. Fall and spring norms (scaled scores, percentile ranks, stanines, grade equivalents), based on a large national sample, are provided.

SRA Achievement Series (by R. A. Naslund, L. P. Thorpe, & D. W. Lefever, Science Research Associates, 1978) These tests measure broad areas of knowledge, general skills, and application. The primary levels (grades K–3) include reading and mathematics (Levels A, B, C, and D) and language arts (Levels C and D). The upper levels (Levels E, F, G, and H for grades 4–12) test these same basic skill areas in addition to social studies, science, and reference materials. Level H also includes a measure of competency in functional or life skills (Survey of Applied Skills). An optional 30-minute test—the Educational Ability Series (EAS), which provides an estimate of educational ability—can be added to all eight achievement levels. Total testing time ranges from 2 hours for Level A to 4 hours, 45 minutes for Level H. The SRA Achievement Series was standardized in the spring of 1978 on a national sample of approximately 83,000 students and in the fall of 1978 on 121,000 students. A variety of norms (grade, percentile, stanine, etc.) based on these two standardizations are reported.

Stanford Achievement Test Series (by E. F. Gardner et al., The Psychological Corporation, 1983) This series of tests, consisting of the Stanford Early School Achievement Test, 2d ed. (SESAT), the Stanford Achievement Tests, 7th ed., and the Stanford Test of Academic Skills, 2d ed. (TASK), provides for comprehensive testing in the basic skills areas (reading, language, mathematics, and so on) from kindergarten through grade 12. The two SESAT levels are designed for grades K.0 through K.9 (SESAT 1) and K.5 through 1.9 (SESAT 2). The six levels of the Stanford Achievement Tests are Primary 1 (grades 1.5–2.9), Primary 2 (grades 2.5–3.9), Primary 3 (grades 3.5–4.9), Intermediate 1 (grades 4.5–5.9), Intermediate 2 (grades 5.5–7.9), and Advanced (grades 7.0–9.9). The two levels of TASK are appropriate for grades 8.0 through 12.9 (TASK 1) and grades 9.0 through 13 (TASK 2). Although students normally would be tested at the corresponding grade levels of the tests, out-of-level testing is possible when the school curriculum is more difficult or easier than the average. The number of subtests included in a particular level of the Stanford Achievement Tests varies from five to eleven. However, most levels of the Stanford Achievement Tests contain subtests of word study skills, reading comprehension, vocabulary, listening comprehension, spelling, language, concepts of number, mathematics computation, and mathematics application. Administration time for the tests on the Stanford Achievement Series ranges from 2 hours, 10 minutes for SESAT 1 to 5 hours, 15 minutes for Intermediate 1 or 2. The entire series was standardized in the fall of 1981 and the spring of 1982 on more than 400,000 schoolchildren. Scaled scores, national percentiles (norms and bands) and achievement-ability comparisons for individuals and entire school classes are provided (see Figure 6–1).

Basic Education Tests Several achievement test batteries have been designed specifically to measure proficiency in basic skills of adults having less than a high school education. One example of a test in this category is the Tests of Adult Basic Education (TABE) (CTB/McGraw-Hill, 1978), an adaptation of the California Achievement Tests assessing skills in reading, mathematics, and language at three levels of difficulty. Another example is the Fundamental Achievement Series (FAS) (by G. K. Bennett and J. E. Doppett, The Psychological Corporation, 1965–1970). The FAS is administered by tape recording and test booklets to adolescents and adults ranging in ability from basic literacy to somewhat above the eighth grade. Three scores are obtained: Verbal (V), Numerical (N), and Verbal + Numerical (V + N). The Verbal and Numerical sections measure practical achievements, such as reading signs and menus, finding numbers or names in a list, recognizing numbers and correctly spelled words, telling time, using calendars, understanding orally presented information, and solving computational problems of varying difficulty.

ACHIEVEMENT TESTS IN SPECIFIC AREAS

The administration of an achievement test battery has first priority in a schoolwide testing program. When more information on pupil achievement in particular areas is desired, the usual procedure is to follow the battery with specific tests in those areas. These specific achievement tests have certain advantages over comparable tests from a battery. For example, the fact that they contain more items and have a wider subject content than a single test from a battery makes it likely that they will represent the instructional objectives of a wider range of teachers and schools.

Hundreds of specific subject-matter tests in reading, mathematics, language, science, social studies, the professions, business, and the skilled trades are available. Other areas in which standardized achievement tests have been constructed are handwriting, health, home economics, industrial arts, library usage, literature, the Bible, music, speech, spelling, and driver education.

Criterion-Referenced and Competency Tests

In addition to the traditional norm-referenced survey, diagnostic, and prognostic instruments, there are many criterion-referenced tests in specific subjects. Furthermore, the current emphasis on basic skills competency testing for high school graduation has led to the publication of a number of proficiency tests for assessing the knowledge and skills of junior and senior high students in reading, writing, and mathematics. These "survival skills," as they have been labeled, are considered essential in coping with the demands of everyday living. Examples of specific subject-matter competency tests at the senior high level are the Senior High Assessment in Reading Performance (SHARP), the Test of Performance in Computational Skills (TOPICS), and the WRITE/Senior High.

Companion instruments at the junior high level include the Performance Assessment in Reading (PAIR), Assessment of Skills in Computation (ASC), and WRITE/Junior High. All of these tests, available from CTB/McGraw-Hill, consist of display-type items representing materials typically encountered in everyday life. It takes approximately two 50-minute class periods to administer a given test, and the results can be used not only for evaluation purposes but also to plan remedial instruction.

Norm-Referenced Reading Tests

Many of the learning difficulties that children experience in school are related to problems in reading. For this reason, it is important to assess reading level and diagnose deficiencies in this subject early and regularly. Because of their many uses, more reading tests are administered than any other type of achievement test. In fact, there are so many reading tests that a separate volume of the Buros series, *Reading Tests and Reviews II* (Buros, 1975), is devoted to them. Various types of reading tests are available, the three major categories being survey tests (most numerous), diagnostic tests, and reading readiness tests.

Survey Reading Tests The main purpose of administering a survey reading test is to determine a person's overall reading ability. These tests include sections of vocabulary items and sections of paragraphs or passages about which questions are asked. A measure of word knowledge is obtained from the vocabulary items, while reading level and speed of reading comprehension are measured from the paragraphs. Two of the most prominent survey reading tests are the Gates-MacGinitie Reading Tests and the Nelson-Denny Reading Tests.

Gates-MacGinitie Reading Tests, 2d ed. (by W. H. MacGinitie, Riverside Publishing Co., 1978) These tests, which are designed for grades 1 through 12, are grouped into seven levels: Basic R (grade 1.0–1.9), Level A (grade 1.5–1.9), Level B (grade 2), Level C (grade 3), Level D (grades 4–6), Level E (grades 7–9), and Level F (grades 10–12). Separate scores on two subtests (Vocabulary and Comprehension) and total are provided at Levels A through F; low, average, or high ratings are given on the letter sounds, Vocabulary, Letter Recognition, and Comprehension subtests at Level R. Testing time is 55 minutes. National norms obtained during 1976–1977 are expressed as grade equivalents, percentile ranks, stanines, normal curve equivalents (NCE), and extended scale scores.

Nelson-Denny Reading Test, Forms C and D (by J. I. Brown, J. M. Bennett, & G. S. Hanna, Riverside Publishing Company, 1981) The range of this test is grades 9–16 and adult. It measures reading ability in terms of vocabulary development, comprehension, and reading rate in two parallel forms (E and F). Regular administration time is 15 minutes for Part I (vocabulary) and 20 minutes for Part II (Comprehension and Rate). The percentile and grade-equivalent norms are based on nationwide samples of approximately 3,500 students per grade in grades 9–12 and several thousand college students. Cut-time (26 minutes) adult norms are also available.

Three other noteworthy survey reading tests are the Gray Oral Reading Tests (pro.ed) for grades 1–12, the Iowa Silent Reading Tests (The Psychological Corporation) for grades 6–12, and the Test of Reading Comprehension (pro.ed) for grades 2–12.

Diagnostic Reading Tests Diagnostic reading tests, which are by far the most common type of diagnostic test, attempt to assess many different factors that affect reading: intelligence, motivation, eye-hand coordination, perceptual ability, and the ability to understand concepts. They contain subtests of word recognition, reading passages, phonetics and pronunciation, silent and oral reading, spelling, and sound discrimination—all for the purpose of discovering the causes of a student's reading disability. Because the correlations among these subtests are often quite high, they do not necessarily represent independent skills. In addition, the reliabilities of the subtests and the test as a whole are frequently not as high as they should be. The following three diagnostic reading tests are representative.

Diagnostic Reading Scales (DRS) (by G. D. Spache, Publishers Test Service, 1972, 1981) The DRS was designed for grades 1 through 8 and senior high students with reading disabilities. There are three word recognition lists, twenty-two reading passages, and twelve word-analysis and phonics tests in this graduated series. The level at which students are introduced to the reading passages depends on their performance on the graded word-recognition lists. Three levels are yielded by the reading passages: instructional level (oral reading), independent level (silent reading), and potential level (auditory comprehension). The word-analysis and phonics tests involve consonants, vowels, syllables, word parts, and word pairs.

Stanford Diagnostic Reading Tests (SDRT): Third Edition (by B. Karlsen & E. F. Gardner, The Psychological Corporation, 1984) This series of tests was designed to measure the reading subskills of comprehension, decoding, and vocabulary at four grade levels, with a measure of rate added at grades 5.0–13. The grade ranges of the four levels of tests are 1.5–3.5 for the Red Level, 2.5–5.5 for the Green Level, 5.0–9.5 for the Brown Level, and 8.5–13 for the Blue Level. The ten different types of tests are classified into four domains: comprehension (word reading, reading comprehension), decoding (auditory discrimination, phonetic analysis, structural analysis), vocabulary (auditory vocabulary, vocabulary, word parts), and rate (reading rate, scanning and skimming). Five to seven of the ten tests are administered at a given level. Testing time ranges from 3 to 40 minutes per test, or a total of 105 minutes for all tests at the Red Level to 116 minutes for all tests at the Blue Level. Two forms, G and H, are available at each level. The SDRT was standardized in the fall of 1983 and spring of 1984; fall and spring norms (percentile ranks, stanines, scaled scores, grade equivalents, normal curve equivalents, and progress indicators) are provided.

Reading Yardsticks (Riverside Publishing Co., 1981) Reading Yardsticks is a criterion-referenced diagnostic reading test for grades K through 8 (Levels 6–14). At Level 6, examinees are tested for visual and auditory discrimination, letter and word matching, vocabulary, and comprehension. At Levels 7–8 they are tested for discrimination and study skills, phonic analysis, vocabulary, and comprehension (also structural analysis at Level 8). At Levels 9–14 vocabulary, comprehension, structural analysis, and study skills are tested. Testing time for the entire battery ranges from 84 minutes at Level 6 to 210 minutes at Levels 10–14.

Reading Readiness Tests As a measure of the extent to which a child possesses the skills and knowledge necessary for learning to read, a reading readiness test often predicts achievement in the first grade better than general intelligence tests such as the Stanford-Binet. For this reason, reading readiness tests, which usually take less time to administer than intelligence tests, may be used when intelligence test scores are not available. Reading readiness tests also contain many of the same types of items as diagnostic reading tests—visual discrimination, auditory blending and discrimination, vocabulary, symbol (letter) recognition, and visual-motor coordination—and are common in kindergarten and first-grade classrooms. Examples of tests in this category are the School Readiness Tests (available from Scholastic Testing Service) and the Metropolitan Readiness Tests.

Metropolitan Readiness Tests (by J. R. Nurss and M. E. McGauvran, The Psychological Corporation, 1976) This group-administered battery, for use in kindergarten or early first grade, consists of two levels of six subtests each. At Level I the subtests are auditory memory, rhyming, letter recognition, visual matching, school language and listening, quantitative language, and an optional copying test. The six prereading subtests at Level II are beginning consonants, sound-letter correspondence, visual matching, finding patterns, school language, listening, and optional subtests on quantitative concepts, quantitative operations, and an optional copying test. Testing time for each level ranges from 80 to 100 minutes. End-of-kindergarten and beginning-first-grade stanines and percentile norms are given.

Mathematics Tests

In a manner similar to achievement tests in reading, mathematics achievement tests may be classified as survey, diagnostic, and prognostic.

Survey Mathematics Tests Since the field of mathematics education has experienced a great deal of change during recent years, a variety of approaches to instruction are represented by current mathematics tests. Certain tests are designed to encompass both modern and traditional emphases in the mathematics curriculum, and instruments reflecting more specialized instructional approaches are also available. In general, survey mathematics tests contain items requiring examinees to demonstrate an understanding of quantitative concepts and operations and the ability to apply this understanding in solving problems. Examples of norm-referenced mathematics tests of the survey type are the End-of-Course Tests in Algebra and Geometry (Publishers Test Service) for students in grades 9–12, the Test of Mathematical Abilities (TOMA), and the Test of Early Mathematics Ability (TEMA).

TOMA and TEMA (pro. ed and Publishers Test Service, 1984) TOMA (by V. L. Brown & E. McEntire), designed for grades 3–10, assesses mathematical skills in solving story problems and performing computations. It also provides information on examinees' attitudes, knowledge of mathematical vocabulary, and general cultural applications. Normative information is given for graded mastery expectations of the 400 basic number facts. TEMA (by H. Ginsburg & A. J. Baroody) consists of a series of items designed to assess the performance of children between 4 and 9 years of age in the domains of formal (knowledge of conventional number facts, calculation, base ten concepts) and informal (concepts of relative magnitude, counting, calculation) mathematics. The standardization samples for both tests were rather small and probably not representative of the population of U.S. schoolchildren in the age ranges of the tests.

Diagnostic Tests in Mathematics Although less widely employed than diagnostic reading tests, diagnostic tests in mathematics also represent an attempt to analyze a complex subject involving a variety of skills into its constituent elements. The items on diagnostic tests of arithmetic and mathematics are based on an analysis of skills and errors in the subject. An excellent example of such a test is the Stanford Diagnostic Mathematics Test. Illustrative of a systems approach in which assessment and instructional materials are combined in a single package are the DMI Mathematics Systems.

Stanford Diagnostic Mathematics Test (by L. S. Beatty, R. Madden & E. F. Gardner, The Psychological Corporation & Bureau of Educational Measurements, 1978) This series of tests was designed to diagnose specific strengths and weaknesses in working with numbers. There are parallel forms, A and B, of the tests at each of four levels. The grade ranges of the four levels are 1.6–4.5 for the Red Level, 3.6–6.5 for the Green Level, 5.6–8.5 for the Brown Level, and 7.6–13 for the Blue Level. Each level consists of tests on number system and numeration, computation, and applications. Total testing time ranges from 1 hour, 30 minutes for the Blue Level to 1 hour, 50 minutes for the Red Level. Percentile ranks, stanines, grade equivalents, and scaled-score norms, in addition to a procedure for objective-referenced interpretation of scores, are provided.

DMI Mathematics Systems (DMI/MS) (by J. K. Gessel, CTB/McGraw-Hill, 1983) Combining diagnostic assessment with instruction in mathematics, the DMI/MS represents a criterion-referenced, diagnostic-prescriptive approach. The system permits a teacher to diagnose a student's instructional needs in mathematics, prescribe appropriate activities, teach specific skills, monitor progress, and reinforce and enrich mastered skills. There are seven levels in the DMI/MS package: A (grades K.6–1.5), B (grades 1.6–2.5), C (grades 2.6–3.5), D (grades 3.6–4.5), E (grades 4.6–5.5), F (grades 5.6–6.5), and G (grades 6.6–8.9+).

Prognostic Tests in Mathematics A number of tests have been designed to forecast performance in specific mathematics courses, but, compared to prognostic tests in reading (reading readiness tests), such tests are not widely administered. An example of prognostic tests in mathematics is the Orleans-Hanna Algebra Prognosis Test–Revised (The Psychological Corporation, 1982) for predicting success in learning algebra. Designed to predict, before instruction begins, which students will be successful and which will encounter difficulties in learning algebra, the Orleans-Hanna assesses aptitude and achievement, as well as interest and motivation. The questionnaire and work sample items on this test take 40 minutes to complete. Percentile rank and stanine score norms for groups of students completing seventh- and eighth-grade mathematics are provided.

Language Tests

Language, as generally construed, refers to any means of communication. Although language tests are primarily of the verbal type, measures of nonverbal communication for use with deaf and, more recently, hearing people have also been designed.

Language is taught at all levels, and tests appropriate for the entire range of grades are available. For example, failure to understand certain concepts can act as a communication barrier between a first-grade pupil and teacher and consequently can have a serious effect on the child's school learning. In recognition of this fact, the Boehm Test of Basic Concepts–Revised (grades K–2) and the Boehm Test of Basic Concepts: Preschool Version (ages 3–5 years) (by A. E. Boehm, The Psychological Corporation, 1986) were designed to measure young children's mastery of basic concepts of space, quantity, and time (Figure 6–2). A kit of materials to help children master the concepts measured by these tests, the *Boehm Resource Guide for Basic Concept Teaching,* is also available from the same publisher.

Despite the existence of tests such as the Boehm, most of the achievement tests listed in the language category are designed for secondary and college students. These instruments, which include both English and foreign language tests, are frequently administered in high schools and colleges for the purpose of placing students in English or foreign language classes appropriate to their level of competence.

English Language Tests Some of the most severe criticisms of objective tests have come from teachers of English, but it is generally recognized that such tests do a fairly respectable job of measuring knowledge of grammar and